Encounters with Quebec:

Emerging Perspectives on Québécois Narrative Fiction

Edited by

Susan L. Rosenstreich

Institute of Global Cultural Studies
Binghamton University
1998

Published by:

Global Publications, IGCS, Binghamton University,
State University of New York, Binghamton,
New York, USA 13902-6000
Phone: (607) 777-4495 or 6104; Fax: (607) 777-6132
E-mail: pmorewed@binghamton.edu

Library of Congress in Publication Data

Susan L. Rosenstreich, *Encounters with Quebec: Emerging Perspectives on Québécois Narrative Fiction*

1. Quebec; 2. Francophone Literature; 3. French Literature;
4. Canadian History; 5. Canadian Literature

ISBN 1-883058-58-9

Encounters with Quebec:
Emerging Perspectives on Québécois Narrative Fiction

Editor
Susan L. Rosenstreich
1998

Table of Contents

Introduction

Susan L. Rosenstreich
Dowling College, New York

Une voix derrière elle déclare avec autorité: <Il faut aller plus loin.>
- Elisabeth Vonarburg, *Les Voyageurs malgré eux*, 87.
[A voice behind her speaks with authority: You must go further.]

As literary creatures and political animals, we ought to concern ourselves with the understanding of human action and the social world as a moment when *something is beyond control, but it is not beyond accommodation.*
- Homi Bhabha, *The Location of Culture,* 12.

Whether Quebec is an old friend or a new acquaintance, reading about its literature has to include at some point a consideration of the place itself. And coming into contact with today's Quebec is not a simple matter. The very name Quebec has become a record of dynamic, at times troubled, meetings of cultures, the consequences of which do not appear to diminish with the passage of time, but which, instead, produce an always more complex identity to match the place name.

The Amerindians, who knew the riverine stretch along the St. Lawrence as *Kebec*, the "place where the waters narrow", witnessed the colonization of their land by the French, fitful at first after Jacques Cartier's initial voyage to the area in 1534, eventually more sustained after Samuel de Champlain established a fortified village in 1608 within the confines of present-day Quebec City. Shortly after the British victory over the troops of General Montcalm on the Plains of Abraham in 1759, Quebec became a shibboleth distinguishing French colonized from British colonizers. Its *habitants*, its *coureurs de bois*, the French farmers and woodsmen of New France, began a two-century struggle to survive, at times desperately, but always purposefully, as a Francophone Catholic island in an Anglophone Protestant sea. The culture of *survivance*, survival as Francophone Catholics at all costs, was hardly a mute accommodation to British imperium. Sociologist Hubert Guindon has challenged the view that, following British victory, Quebec society withdrew immediately into rural isolation and stagnation. He offers English-language readers instead an image of a Quebec that continued to adapt and change from 1760 to 1960, political appearances frequently to the contrary, in his essay "The Social Evolution of Quebec Reconsidered".[1]

The victory of the Liberal Party in 1960 ended "the time of the nationalism of submission and powerlessness that defined Quebec as a rural, clerical society" (Monière 288), and launched the *Révolution tranquille*, the quiet revolution that transformed Quebec into a statist urbanizing polity in little less than six years. As an indication of the importance placed on Quebec's language, history and arts, so zealously nurtured over two centuries, Article One of the Liberal Party's 1960 Manifesto called for the creation of a department of cultural affairs.[2]

But the rise of the Front de libération du Quebec, a "revolutionary movement" (Regush 4), officially launched in 1963 with the goal of organizing labor against capitalism, made it clear that the revolution would not proceed quietly. The FLQ's perception that "Quebec workers were being oppressed and exploited by the English-Canadian bourgeoisie and American imperialists" (Monière 268) fueled the October Crisis of 1970. By the end of that fatal month Quebec had changed. Paul Cross, a British trade commissioner in Montreal, was being held hostage by members of the FLQ. Ottawa had invoked the War Measures Act, claiming the need to ensure public safety in Quebec. Parliament had simultaneously approved Public Order Regulations 1970 for the province, declaring the FLQ an illegal organization. As a result, at least 250 individuals had been arrested. (By the end of the year 468 would be jailed, of which 408 would be released without charges being brought.) And Pierre Laporte, minister of labor and immigration for Robert Bourassa's government in Quebec, a second hostage of the FLQ, had been executed by the movement's Dieppe cell.[3]

The crisis subsided with the release of Cross and the arrests of Laporte's executioners, but the debate showed no signs of diminishing. Opposition parties in Ottawa added their voices to those in Quebec who were skeptical of the "alleged insurrection" which had led to the implementation of the War Measures Act; the Canadian Civil Liberties Association called the Public Order Act unnecessary and repressive; Canada's Prime Minister Trudeau was accused of imposing his will on Quebec's Prime Minister Bourassa. "Who governed Quebec?" this debate asked. Were the people of Quebec self-determined, or were they puppets of Ottawa? Certainly from the perspective of the last years of this century,

> "the October Crisis was a turning point in Canadian history. Superficially it forced a re-examination of Quebec nationalism, and the relations between Quebec and the rest of Canada. Far more important, however, it forced a re-examination of fundamental attitudes, beliefs, and values. The nationalism of the FLQ might be limited and contained; its radicalism brought Canada fully into the last half of the century, for it challenged less the existence of the nation-state than the nature of the society within it" (Saywell 152).

The referendum of 1980, asking Quebec if it wished its leaders to negotiate "sovereignty" with Ottawa,[4] carried 40.44 per cent of the vote.[5] By way of comparison, in the 1995 referendum on sovereignty, for which 93 per cent of eligible voters turned out, 49.4 per cent supported the option for independence. Premier Jacques Parizeau, whose Parti Québécois led the secessionist campaign, attributed the slim victory against sovereignty to big business and the immigrant vote.

Today's Quebec recalls these meetings with Others, and its aspirations as a distinct culture and dynamic representations of its difference refer to this history. As Monique Lafortune implies in *Le Roman québécois: reflet d'une société*, literature, or at least the novel, represents a society to itself and to the rest of the reading world. Thus, as events have propelled Quebec toward its various embodiments---territory, colony, province, and now province imagining sovereign status---perspectives on its literature have shifted and adjusted as literary criticism performs its task of perceiving changes in the self-representation of the society behind the text.

For nearly two centuries, Quebec authors were told that "une littérature québécoise était possible dans le langage de Marcel Proust pourvu que le regard demeurât indigène sur une réalité d'Amérique" (Dorion, Voisin 27) [a Québécois literature was possible in the language of Marcel Proust provided that its viewpoint remained a native one, focused on a (North) American reality]. But this view was overshadowed by events in the mid-sixties, such as the 1965 production of Michel Tremblay's *Les Belles-Soeurs*. Performed in Quebec's "joual" variant of French, the play put onstage characters who spoke what one might hear in Montreal, not in Paris, a sure sign that, for Quebec, literature no longer had "le statut d'objet á imiter, mais d'objet á s'approprier" (Dorion, Voisin 28) [the status of an object to imitate, but an object to appropriate]. Critics would no longer evaluate literature as "an instrument for advancing a particular ideology", but would turn to interpretation, resulting in "an unprecedented variety of critical approaches, all of which combine to present a view of Quebec literature in its full diversity" (Shouldice 8).

It is appropriate, then, that essays in a collection on contemporary narrative fiction in Quebec view their subject through perspectives that seek to illuminate that "full diversity". In one way or another, but not in any single way other than in their provenance, the works of narrative fiction examined on the following pages are seen to be Québécois. They reflect distinct realities that belong to Quebec, with all the representations of reality that site can offer. It has been the concern of the essayists to develop and focus their insights on Québécois fiction so that the diversity of its realities brings the reader closer to present-day Quebec.

Two essays, each focusing on a well-established contemporary Quebec author, open the collection. These fresh interpretations of writers familiar to experienced readers of Quebec fiction are also eminently accessible introductions for more casual readers. Although the figure of gardens in Anne Hébert's work has been considered by others,[6] Janis Pallister approaches the subject through the paradigm of mother-daughter bonds, reaching into Hébert's texts for keys to their complex layering of Classical and Biblical allusions. In so doing, she contributes to the line of inquiry followed by such scholars as Victor-Laurent Tremblay, uncovering a possible "ossature", a framework as Tremblay calls it, (Tremblay 2) within Hébert's prose.

Through the work of Jacques Poulin, Ritt Deitz tracks phases in Quebec's changing identity and self-representation since the end of the Quiet Revolution. His essay might bring to mind aspects of Hubert Aquin's concept of literature, alluded to in the title of a collection of essays by that author in English translation, *Writing Quebec: Selected Essays*. Deitz's focus on Poulin's central characters in this essay advances a neo-heroic view of the individual, supported by the notion that "le drame le plus personnel, le plus intime, ne saurait se détacher du drame collectif" (Dorion, Voisin 235), [the most personal, the most intimate drama, cannot be detached from the collective drama]. This essay also draws attention to the tension between inward/backward and outward/forward gazes in Québécois narrative fiction, and Deitz's discussion of "américanité", an expanded North American consciousness, in Poulin's *Volkswagen Blues* serves as a transition to explications of this tension in the succeeding essays.

The diachronic survey of the machine as metaphor in Québécois fiction, which opens Jean-François Chassay's essay "Progress and its Paradoxes", acquaints readers with a central concern in the literature of Quebec: will the past be lost if progress is gained? "Je me souviens" --- I remember, declare Quebec license plates. Why would one forget? The power of technology to induce change and erase borders makes it a fearful adversary of memory and mass, as Chassay demonstrates, yet he goes on to show how Québécois novelists have used technology in their fiction to introduce plasticity and resilience into always already structured world views. In this respect, the essay contributes to the context of a discussion on the evolution of the conceptual individual into the post-modern subject, the nature of which has been suggested by such works as *Modernité/Postmodernité du roman contemporain,* under the direction of Madeleine Frédéric and Jacques Collard, and by Janet M. Paterson's critique of that topic in *Postmodernism and the Quebec Novel.* Chassay's study of technology in narrative fiction gives further evidence of the increasing interpenetration of the social sciences and literature.

Guy Teissier's piece on the trope of identity in recent Quebec theatre expands upon the post-modern subject, this time through an examination of authors. In a dialectic trajectory that bounces from literary text to performance to author, or, in this case, playwright, back to text once again, the essay supports the reputation of Québécois theatre as the force that impels narrative fiction to its "point de vertige" (Dorion, Voisin 30), the point of vertigo where fiction and the real world whirl inextricably into a single spectacle. As in the essays by Deitz and Chassay, identity as an individual issue as well as a collective one figures prominently in this assessment of the concern of Québécois authors for how reality, from which identity proceeds, is constituted.

The exploration of the problematics of identity, the introverted and extroverted itineraries it follows in Quebec, continues in Ramon Hathorn's study of Neo-Québécois authors, a term that refers here to immigrant writers, as well as to second generation Québécois authors. Introducing his discussion with a diachronic survey of the early Quebec novel, he perceives a literary watershed in the works of "master storyteller" Yves Thériault, a Quebec novelist[7] with an interest in marginalized cultural minorities. But, as Hathorn notes, Neo-Québécois writers bring pasts quite unlike that of Thériault to their work, and they alter the link between fiction and real experience as a consequence. He demonstrates how the past, a subject of substantial importance in Leslie Laczko's study, *Pluralism and Inequality in* Quebec, and in Winfried Siemerling's *Writing Ethnicity: Cross-Cultural Consciousness in Canadian and Québécoise Literature*, ramifies through the narration of the author with an immigrant or culturally marginal heritage. Even as this anthology is being edited, such modifications of Quebec's literary landscape are having a significant impact on the evolution of the province's metanarrative.

The nature of that impact is suggested by the closing two essays of the book, in each of which there is one author who has already been introduced by Ramon Hathorn. In contrast with Hathorn's, are synchronic studies that bring us face to face with the influx of "écriture migrante", the literature of ethnic writers living and working in Quebec. Susan Ireland's study of changes in the relationships between mothers and daughters depicted by several Neo-Québécoises authors recalls, in terms of subject matter, the opening essay of the collection. But the contrast in the two perspectives serves as a marker in this book's range of views. Building on recent feminist inquiries into mother-daughter bonds, Ireland sees radical revisions in Neo-Québécoises fictional representations of them. The change stems from new views of the formation of female personal identities, developed as a consequence of Neo-Québécoises authors' personal experiences, and offers fresh hope for Québécois literature as a catalyst in social transformation.

Peter Klaus has the final word, his essay on Latino-Québécois writers offering a case study approach for the development of perspectives in the study of Quebec's literature. The value of this particular Neo-Québécois literature has been in offering a forum to express, and at times to resolve, the universal trauma of exile, shaping, perhaps even reshaping, language in the process. Beyond that, the presence of Latino-Québécois narrative fiction in Quebec poses the problem of how that fiction will participate in literary life there. Will its authors devote their energy to the voicing of identities, and abandon story-telling? Is this the beginning of another literature, one in which, as Régine Robin predicts in *La Québécoite*, "(I)l n'y aura pas de récit/ tout juste une voix plurielle/ une voix carrefour/ la parole immigrante" (Robin 90) [There will be no story/

just a plural voice/ a crossroads voice/ the spoken immigrant word]? In a rapidly evolving Quebec, where answers are far from certain, the only certainty is that the act of remembering and the gesture of writing will continue to be linked through identity in Québécois narrative fiction.

Before closing, some explanations are in order. The essays in this book were collected with the English-speaking newcomer to Quebec studies in mind. Therefore, we have relied, where feasible, on background works available in English, in the introduction as well as in the additional reading lists included in endnotes or appended at the end of the essays. For those whose French needs support, the essayists have translated citations from the French into English. Exceptionally, translations of citations in the article by Jean-François Chassay are by Eric de Larochellière, and those in Guy Teissier's article are mine. Translations of titles mentioned in the essays are literal where the work has not yet been translated. When the work has been translated, the title of the English version appears in italics. Titles composed solely of proper nouns have not been translated. Orthography being part of the debate surrounding Francophone culture in Quebec, we have respected authors' variations in the anglicized spelling of the adjective *Québécois*.

A collection of essays is the work of many minds, and to the editor falls the welcome chance to thank individuals who collaborated in the making of this book. Above all, thanks are due the contributors. They patiently observed the troublesome guidelines for essays, and struggled to comply with due dates, managing all the while to express original and seminal viewpoints. The contributors and I are indebted to Maureen Volpe for the unstinting amount of time and energy she devoted to editing tasks, and to Jeannine Sandrini-Cooke, whose eagle eye caught the false friends hiding in the text. The support of library staffs was invaluable, and as editor, I am particularly grateful to librarians at Dowling College, the Suffolk County Library System, the Feinberg Library of the State University of New York at Plattsburgh, and the University of Vermont in Burlington. A special expression of appreciation goes to Dr. Jeanne Kissner and Dr. Richard Beach, co-directors of the Center for the Study of Canada in Plattsburgh, whose hospitable orientation saved days of valuable editing time. I thank also my colleagues at the Dowling College Press for their support of this anthology. Finally, I take this opportunity to recognize my debt to my grandparents, who inspired the project on Francophone narrative fiction of which this book is a part. I continue to be in awe of their determination to overcome obstacles of time, distance, and language so that they might share, through stories, their fearlessness of the past, and their engagement with an ever-emerging, always mysterious future.

Works Cited and Bibliography

Actes du Colloque de l'Université du Québec à Montréal, under the direction of Madeleine Frédéric and Jacques Collard. Montreal: Presses de l'Université du Québec à Montréal, 1985.

Aquin, Hubert. *Writing Quebec: Selected Essays*. University of Alberta Press, 1988.

Bhabha, Homi K. *The Location of Culture*. London, New York: Routledge, 1994.

Dorion, Gilles and Marcel Voisin, Editors. *Littérature québécoise: voix d'un peuple, voies d'une autonomie*. Brussels: Editions de l'Université de Bruxelles, 1985.

Guindon, Hubert. *Quebec Society: Tradition, Modernity, and Nationhood*. Introduction by Roberta Hamilton and John L. McMullan. Toronto: University of Toronto Press, 1988.

Hesse, M. G. *Yves Thériault, Master Storyteller*. New York: Peter Lang, 1993.

Knight, Kelton. *Anne Hébert: In Search of the First Garden*. New York: Peter Lang, 1995.

Lazko, Leslie. *Pluralism and Inequality in Quebec*. New York: St. Martin's Press, 1995.

Lafortune, Monique. *Le Roman québécois: reflet d'une société*. Laval: Mondia, 1985.

Monière, Denis. *Ideologies in Quebec: The Historical Development*. Toronto: University of Toronto Press, 1981. Chapters 1 through 8 translated from Denis Monière, *Le Développement des idéologies au Québec: des origines à nos jours*. Montreal: Editions Québec/Amérique, 1977.

Paterson, Janet M., David Homel and Charles Phillips. *Postmodernism and the Quebec Novel*. Buffalo, Toronto: University of Toronto Press, 1994.

Quinn, Herbert F. *The Union Nationale: A Study in Quebec Nationalism*. Toronto: University of Toronto Press, 1963.

Regush, Nicholas M. *Pierre Vallières: The Revolutionary Process in Quebec*. New York: The Dial Press, 1973.

Robin, Régine. *La Québécoite*. Montreal: Québec/Amérique, 1993.

Saywell, John. *Quebec 70: A Documentary Narrative*. Toronto: University of Toronto Press, 1971. Reprinted from *Canadian Annual Review for 1970*.

Shouldice, Larry. *Contemporary Quebec Criticism*. Toronto: University of Toronto Press, 1979.

Siemerling, Winfried, Editor. *Writing Ethnicity: Cross-cultural Consciousness in Canadian and Québécoise Literature*. Toronto: ECW Press, 1996.

Tremblay, Victor-Laurent. *Au Commencement était le mythe*. Ottawa: Presses Universitaires d'Ottawa, 1991.

The Americana Annual. Grolier Incorporated: 1981 and 1996.

Vonarberg, Elisabeth. *Les Voyageurs malgré eux*. Montreal: Editions Québec-Amérique, 1994.

Endnotes

1. In *Quebec Society: Tradition, Modernity, and Nationhood*, Hubert Guindon; Introduction by Roberta Hamilton and John L. McMullan; Toronto: University of Toronto Press, 1988.

2. See Appendix C, "1960 Political Manifesto of the Quebec Liberal Party" in *The Union Nationale: A Study in Quebec Nationalism*, Herbert F. Quinn; Toronto: University of Toronto Press, 1963.

3. In a November 12 statement before the National Assembly, Justice Minister Jérôme Choquette referred to Communiqué Number 6 from the Chenier cell, in which it was announced that the Dieppe cell had carried out the execution (Saywell 141). Paul and Jacques Rose and Francis Simard, eventually convicted of Laporte's murder, were said to be members of the Chenier cell (Saywell 55).

4. See English text of the referendum put before Quebec voters in 1980, in *The Americana Annual, 1981*, Grolier Incorporated, 1981; 172.

5. In *The Americana Annual, 1996*, the vote is reported to have been 42 per cent in favor.

6. See, for example, *Anne Hébert: In Search of the First Garden*, Kelton Knight, 1997.

7. See, *Yves Thériault, Master Storyteller,* M.G. Hesse. New York: Peter Lang, 1993.

On Mothers, Daughters, and Gardens in the Writings of Anne Hébert

Janis L. Pallister
Bowling Green State University, Ohio

The intention of this essay is to examine the relationship of mothers and daughters in selected works of Anne Hébert, one of Quebec's most celebrated novelists. If gardens are involved in the question, it is because ultimately we must think of the "first garden" which she and others refer to as "the womb." In addition, we must understand allusions to the "first garden" as referring not only to kindergarten or childhood, but also to Quebec itself, and to the first gardens planted by the colonists in Nouvelle France, so long ago. These themes are all quite apparent in one of Hébert's more recent novels, *Le Premier Jardin* (1988) [*The First Garden*]; but in previous novels the complexities of the relationship of mother and daughter, as well as the behavior of the phallic or darkly evil mother, were already being examined. Especially is this true of her novels *Kamouraska* (1970) and *Les Fous de Bassan* (1982) [*In The Shadow of the Wind*]. Additionally, in this latter novel we may appreciate the extent to which Hébert can dip into ancient myths from Greece and from the Bible to reinforce the themes of motherhood and even to explode them. She will continue these allusions and explosions in *Le Premier Jardin.*

In *Le Premier Jardin,* Flora, an aging actress returns from France to her native Quebec, where she not only reminisces but also is haunted by a terrible catastrophe of her childhood and a generous dose of guilt.

The guilt of Flora, protagonist of *Le Premier Jardin*, is easily the issue of a fundamentally old-style Catholic society's stereotypical concept of woman, as the symbolism and content of the novel show. The novel continues the portrayal of the witch mother of Hébert's *Enfants du Sabbat* [*Children of the Black Sabbath*] and of the phallic mother of her *Fous de Bassan:* Here in *Le Premier Jardin* we have allusions to the *vampire-actrice* (81) [actress-vampire], an actress who lives off other people's stories, one who plays Phèdre the stepmother,[1] the phallic mother brought to the stage through image acting (mimesis) and lived in reality by the guilt-ridden Flora (whose name also evokes the bride of spring, another first mother). Mythological and literary allusions are multiplied through the search for the unknown mother [*la mère inconnue*] (100-101) and for the lost daughter [*la fille perdue*] (Maud; Fantine of *Les Misérables*; Pierrette caught in the snow; Winnie caught in the sand). Flora's search for the lost mother reminds us of the search of Telemachus for his lost father, while the literary allusions to Hugo and to Beckett evoke the bitter experience of the orphaned and marginalized.

These evocations can be seen to prolong the references to Demeter, the great mother goddess of Greek mythology and her daughter Persephone, already richly present through the grandmother and the two girls, Nora and Olivia, of *Les Fous de Bassan.*[2] But to some of the characters, the mother-grandmother of *Les Fous...*was a phallic mother, a false grandmother as well. We shall return to these matters later. Meanwhile, let us stress that such a grandmother is not absent from *Le Premier Jardin;* we have constant references to the false grandmother and false granddaughter, to the real mother and the real daughter ["la fausse grand'mère," "la fausse petite-fille" and "la vraie fille," "la vraie mère"] (160), not to mention the nuns of the hospice, called in French *la bonne soeur/mère* (i.e., sister or mother superior, which is preceded by the word 'good' in French). The stepmother (the *belle-mère,* the *mauvaise mère*) is ever present, haunting the *fille adoptive* [adopted daughter]: witness the stepmothers of Pierrette, of Guillemette, and of Flora. And where mother fails as mother, she is artist, "mother of all her 'roles'." She can delight in her maternity: it can be thought of as a "*fusion amoureuse*" [bonding through love]; one can revel in the "*odeur de la mère*" [smell of the mother]; one can experience the joy of being/becoming a mother (110-11). Such are the polar opposites on which the novel is constructed.

We should look, too, to Eve, the first mother, first daughter, as well; to Eve, the spoiler, in the first garden (Eden), site of original sin (lost paradise) --- a constant preoccupation of Hébert. This was the sin of which Mary was free; thus the nuns of *Les Enfants*....put themselves under the vocable of the Immaculate Conception. In *Le Premier Jardin,* the tree of forbidden fruit is transformed to *femme-arbre; arbre généalogique* [a woman-tree or tree-woman; a genealogical tree](124). Eve is first mother, Flora, first bride of Spring, Aurore --- dawn, the little maid of Hébert's novel, raped and murdered; but also child martyr and victim of the evil stepmother in terms of Quebec's literature and cinema. The relationship of the cruel stepmother to the innocent stepchild is especially notable, for example, in a classic film entitled, *La Petite Aurore, l'enfant martyre* (1951) [*Little Aurore, child martyr*]. In that film, as also in *Le Premier Jardin,* the martyred child evolves into the symbol of Quebec's suffering under foreign English oppression. (See 71; 97-8; 100.) Note this evolution in the metaphor whereby the First Garden stood naked in that Dawn, at the very beginning of the world, "before the English conquest" (95). Note, too, by analogy, that in *Kamouraska*, Elisabeth is "chased" from her dying husband's room (trans., 25) like a guilty sinner being driven from Eden, or like a criminal pursued by justice, or like an animal tricked by a hunter. The metaphor of the chase or the hunt is very common in the works of Hébert, and is applied to Antoine Tassy in *Kamouraska* (trans., 62), as it is to the two cousins in *Les Fous de Bassan.*

Tangentially, let us note that Anne Hébert has written two stunning poems about our great mother Eve that provide insight into the confraternity of deadly sin, and, as one of them appears in the collection *Le Mystère de la parole* [Mystery of the Word], we must attempt to see the link between them and the poetic if not the theological Word or Logos. The prayer to Eve in *Le Mystère de la parole* suggests the link. While Eve is the source of sin --- sin, the ally of her powerful beauty --- she is also a primogenetrix and the "Mother of Christ," as of us all. This latter interpretation is borne out by the poem about Eve found in the collection *Les Songes en équilibre* [Poems in Balance], where she is equated with the beginning of the world, with primordial reptilian life, with springtime, and, above all, with the song in the poet's own heart --- a song made up of three words or notes: *Petite Eve Intacte*/or *Plainte, Appel*, and *Séduction* (142-3). These can be said to constitute three major branches of lyric poetry, and, more profoundly, three stages of the fall, or of any fall, and equally the "trois coups de la création du monde" [three strokes of the creation of the world], mentioned in yet another poem. (Ironically fall and creation are bound together.) Quintessentially, Eve is intact and a *chant* is brought back from the Blake-like experience.

One must not overlook, either, the fact that the very title *Le Premier Jardin* bears reflections of Eden, as well as of "kindergarten" --- or childhood (Flora's in the orphanage; the formative experience of the fire, the foster mother) --- and so forth. The novel is specifically reflective of the notion that the first garden was Quebec (City) --- peopled by the "*filles du roi*" [daughters of the king] (see 95; 100). This refers, of course, to that well known group of women --- strong and healthy --- sent by the French king to be wives of the first settlers of Quebec. Ironically they are the "daughters" of the king. All of these women, like little Renée Chauvreaux, experienced their *Premier Jardin* (104) --- in which the tragedies of mother and daughter unfold(ed).

Hébert tells us that the First Garden, Eden, was Old Quebec; Louis Hébert was the first man, Adam, and Marie Rollet, the first woman, or specifically, "premiére mère; mère du pays" (79) [first mother; mother of the country], Eve. Of course, in history books we may read a more elaborate explanation: Louis Hébert was an apothecary who arrived with Poutrincourt's expedition of 1606, one of the first settlements at Port Royal in present-day Nova Scotia. And Marie Rollet was his wife. (See Jones's *Gentlemen and Jesuits.*) Parenthetically, the autobiographical allusion to the author's own ancestry does not escape us.

In the first garden of New France, this couple planted seeds from France; indeed, you would have taken it for a garden in France --- and the first apple tree was brought from Acadie. The Old; the Young; the Old, the New. The New World transformed them. The very image of the Old World, of the Motherland, of France, and of Touraine --- the garden of France (35) --- like Flora's own mother --- was *effacée* (76-77) [lost; erased]. But the sense of original sin seems also effaced from this version of the First Garden. For in fact, the first human to look on this garden was not that couple --- Adam and Eve, or Louis Hébert and Marie Rollet. --- but an Amerindian; and what did he know of original sin? This was the white man's myth; it came to these virgin shores on his boats, together with his canons, his toilet water, his holy water (79).

The story of Flora and Maud, largely a story of a mother and daughter who have been separated, is, in a sense, also the story of France (mother) and Quebec (daughter); to some extent both are reconciled at the end of the tale --- yet they will always be separated, will they not? (And the fact that Anne Hébert herself has always floated between the two countries both physically and spiritually, as well as artistically, may have definite bearing on the story, too.[3] That is, the novel may have many autobiographical referents, though Anne Hébert denies this.)

Flora's return to the *Premier Jardin*, to Quebec, to her *motherland* or in French, to the *"ville-pays-mère,"* is not only a return to the site of her traumatic childhood, to "kindergarten," to the hospice, but it is also and by nature of the fact that Quebec is the place where she passed her earliest years, a return to the second womb. It is consequently the occasion of a second, if not third, expulsion, also.

Le Premier Jardin is a study in exile, loneliness, in the epistemology of loss: it is a tale of separation and erasure. All of these mothers and stepmothers, daughters and stepdaughters, archetypal grandmothers --- all are fused together; all are nameless. Women, whatever they undergo, will lose their names: through the convent, through marriage, by becoming someone's maid (116); by being an orphan (131; 137). Women lose their identity, too, by playing a role: Flora (Phèdre-Winnie) will play Mme Frola, anagram for Flora, on her return to Paris. Identity is lost as well through other aspects of one's art: by taking a stage name, for example, and by assuming the identities of all the female characters one plays/has played, if one is an actress: "Hedda Gabler, Adrienne Lecouvreur, Marie Tudor, Yerma, Phèdre, Mlle Julie" (50). Additionally, "...elle s'échappait d'elle-même pour devenir tout à l'intérieur d'elle-même"(153) [she is Winnie deep inside herself]. By being the "mother" to the "role" which is her "baby" --- she brings the character "to life" but loses her own "life" (174).

We said the separation of Old World and New was forever. But is it? Ruth Mésavage finds that a reconciliation takes place between Flora and her past as well as between Flora and Maud: "France and Quebec, mother and daughter, thus do they symbolically reconcile their personal history to that of their country." This reconciliation ostensibly stirs Flora's creative inspiration: "Flora Fontanges découvre le lien qui la rattache à la mythologie de son pays. Sa réintégration dans l'univers féminin prépare un nouveau centre spirituel qui signale la régénération de l'actrice et de sa créativité artistique" (Mésavage 77), [Flora Fontanges discovers the bond that connects her to the mythology of her country. Her reintegration into the feminine universe prepares a new spiritual center that signals the regeneration of the actress and of her artistic creativity.] But is this true? The Old World culture, built from the time of the Greeks forward on male prerogatives, as Louky Bersianik so brilliantly demonstrates in her *Piquenique sur l'Acropole,* [Picnic on the Acropolis], seems ever ready to spring forth. This is demonstrated by the question raised in *Le Premier Jardin* as to whether Québécoises actresses and/or women authors can even write their own lines. Or must they needs fall back upon the words of French poets (such as Paul Verlaine) to express themselves? This rather crucial question surfaces when Anne Hébert/Flora describes the reaction of the audience to Beckett's play: "On leur a sans doute déjà parlé du corps et de l'âme délétères...et les sanglots longs des violons berçaient leurs coeurs" (a paraphrase from one of Verlaine's most famous poems).

Whether the separation from the Old World is complete or not is one matter; what is most at issue in *Le Premier Jardin* seems to be the mother-daughter bonding, or lack thereof, in all its many forms. Cathexis in the mother-daughter relationship is, for feminist thinkers such as Adrienne Rich, essential, distorted, misused; it is, in fact, "the great unwritten story." One may contend, however, that the themes of mother-grandmother-stepmother-sister as related to daughter-granddaughter-stepdaughter-sister or cousin --- often presented as a form of cathexis --- are widely explored in Quebec literature and film. Such explanations would include *Bonheur d'occasion,* [*The Tin Flute*]*; La Petite Aurore; Les Bons Débarras* [*Good Riddance*]; *Maria Chapdelaine;* and many works by writers of generations younger than Hébert, including *Night Cows* of Jovette Marchessault, not to mention certain works of Nicole Brossard and Louky Bersianik, or the searing words of Isabelle to her mother Marie-Jeanne, in France Vézina's *Androgyne.* The themes of relationships often take on the traditional love-hate, allegiance-betrayal structures present in the historical and contemporary exchanges between France and Quebec, or the oppression visited by England upon Quebec. One may claim, too, that Anne Hébert alone has written several chapters of that story through her novels: *Kamouraska,* in which Elizabeth has complex reactions to her domineering aunts and mother, as well as to her "terrible" mother-in-law; *Les Enfants du sabbat,* in which the chief protagonist floats between mystic bonding with the mother-superior and deeds of witchcraft involving not only sisters in the convent but also her brother whose wife she hates --- all this following a strange upbringing with her mother and father, who hold outright witches' sabbaths including perverted sexual acts; *Les Fous de Bassan,* in which virtually all the action and much of the longing is tied to the largely undesirable mother figures and to the archetypal grandmother, and, especially *Le Premier Jardin,* where the mother-daughter relationship is not only vital to Flora, the central character, but takes on Christian and mythological proportions (just as *Les Fous de Bassan,* and also *Héloïse* rest partially -- - and respectively --- on the Greek myths or Demeter and Orpheus).

Indeed, variations on the mother-daughter topos in Anne Hébert's novels extend further into sister-to-sister, or cousin-to-cousin (even cousin german) relationships. These, of course, simulate the structures of the mother-daughter relationship. The connections tying father to daughter and brother to sister are less common, but nevertheless present, in Hébert's writings: witness Olivia's slavish relationship to her father and brothers in *Les Fous de Bassan.* Her mother being dead, perhaps even murdered by her father, she has become the housekeeper and prisoner of these men.

Thus, Hébert's story bears the marks of both the Adonis-Demeter myth and the Hades-Demeter myth, although perhaps these analogies are only accidental on the part of the novelist. (Hades, by the way, had also seduced his concubine-to-be Mintha, who clashes with the Demeter-Persephone couple and attempts to short-circuit that relationship [Mintha-Maureen?].) After Hades' abduction and rape of Persephone, Persephone's mother Demeter, to gain revenge, laid waste to the land. How often Hébert insists upon the ravage and waste that befell the site of her story, Griffin Creek, after the tragic events of 31 August, 1936. (See Hébert, 1982, 233).

Yet, in the novel the myth is exploded at the juncture of the death of Persephone dédoublée, or Persephone flanked by Artemis. As in the myth, Nora and Olivia disappear on the last night of summer (162), when the moon is full (August 31), after which it is autumn (180) and then November (193). Nora-Artemis, goddess of the moon, fully describes this moon as it becomes orange --- a harvest moon --- and then wanes (135). If our story ends in the fall, it will be remembered that Persephone had been given fruit so as to scatter the seeds. They were stored underground after the harvest; and Persephone was to come back to Hades for a third of the year, in the winter, and then was to return to earth in the spring, and stay through the summer.

But Hébert undermines the myth: the young maidens of the novel will not return in the spring, indeed not ever, despite the fact that the seed of the pomegranate has been provided, here in the form of an apple eaten by Nora, who spits out the seeds, from which she thinks that orchards will spring up (112); and also in the form of apples offered to the girls --- just before their death --- from off Maureen's twisted trees, the ones that had blossomed pink and white in the springtime (65; 134; 157), but at the end of the "story" are dead (199). The wasteland is permanent. The spirituality of the community is also dried up: for in Jungian terms, the dead woman means the death of the anima (Jung, *Man and his Symbols*). Her disembodied voice may give us only cold comfort; at best it is a sterile sign of that immortality once associated with Demeter and her daughter Persephone. (Olivia achieves speech after death --- how proper to the status of women in North American, or better Western, society!)

Nor should this analogy of the novel with the story of Persephone and Demeter come as any surprise, for we have encountered this chthonic or subterranean focus and this replication of myth in any number of Hébert's writings, as for instance her collection of poems, *Le Tombeau des rois,* [tomb of the kings] and in her orphic novella, *Héloise.* (See Bibliography, Pallister, "Orphic...Héloïse.")

Whether we consider Felicity, the grandmother of *Les Fous...*, to be associated with Demeter or not, the fact remains that for Nicolas Jones her son and for Stevens her grandson, Felicity is the phallic mother who has virtually incapacitated them. Stevens remembers that she has said that "tous les hommes sont des cochons..." (75), [all men are pigs] and both the pastor, who spies on his mother (35; 38), and Stevens say that she has "toujours préféré les filles..." (37;75) [always preferred girls]. But the references to the grandmother Felicity--references made in the novel by the pastor, Stevens, and the maidens --- serve also to highlight the notion of the women as sea-allies, and to outline a *mythic matriarchal goddess*. She is referred to once in the novel as "une reine offensée (34) [an offended queen]; and elsewhere as "une méduse géante" (35) [a giant medusa] --- probably with no debt to the meditations of Cixous on that subject. In any case, the grandmother is additionally, as I hinted above, the *primal mother*, through whom all the characters are somehow related. She is also the ancient earth-goddess, the mother goddess, the goddess mother of all, i.e. the mythical mother, of basic matter, embodied as well in the figure of Eve, previous to, and innocent of, original sin --- a figure Hébert returns to over and over in her writings, and in particular in *Le Premier Jardin* (76-77; 100; 124; etc.). This earth-goddess and her co-maiden(s) (the kora/koras) represent the female body, which is time and space. The earth is the body of the goddess, and the goddess, like the earth, is total containment, androgynous, and tied to the moon, which dies like the female egg and is resurrected every month. She (Felicity) is, here, as in some versions of the myth, tied to the sea and also to the land. She can walk on water, Perceval thinks (151). Of course, the sea and its tides are also under the "spell" of the (feminine) moon. The moon, as I said, was under the sign of Artemis, goddess of hunt, childbirth and moon (Nora). To the extent that the pastor and Stevens overthrow this goddess, or these goddesses, we have a re-enactment in the novel of the patriarchal pseudo-Christian overtaking the earth-goddess. (See 2nd letter of *Peter,* where her overthrow is announced; also Joseph Campbell's writings.)

What is most salient, of course, is Hébert's persistent return to the relationship of the mother and daughter, both on the mythic level and on the level of the novel per se (be it *Les Fous* --- or *Le Premier Jardin*); and this powerful bonding is poignantly shown in the final passage of *Les Fous* --- where the dead Olivia hears the voice of her mother (and of all her grandmothers --- avatars of the mother), warning of the dangers inherent in her association with Stevens Brown. Did not Elisabeth's mother make similar statements in *Kamouraska?* Karen McPherson[4] shows not only how Thanatos and Eros are interlocked, but how that very phenomenon is a virtual reality in the experience of marriage and death (McPherson 64). She also shows how the greatest "enemies" to the Hebertian "heroine" are women, as is well illustrated in *Kamouraska* by the role of Aurélie. (Note how Elisabeth often calls Aurélie her "sister" --- yet the appellation has a current of irony, to say the least. (ex., trans., 71; 179; 183). Indeed sisterhood, which is tangential but clearly pertinent to our present consideration of mother-daughter bonding, is undermined more often than not by the women's relationships to a man or to men. If, as McPherson contends, this is true of *Kamouraska,* how much more true it is of *Les Fous de Bassan*, where rivalries are set up between the two cousins (double cousins and, therefore, veritable sisters) when Stevens Brown enters the picture.

Even more tellingly, McPherson, in her study of *Kamouraska* (120 ff), shows Elisabeth's considerable debt to her mother, who is catalyst, in fact, to many of her conflicts: from her mother has come her whole heritage. Her father being dead, it is her mother, assisted by her aunts (see trans., 40-43; 51 passim), who tends to her Catholic religion, with its accompanying moral law; makes her conscious of her class; of her family honor. And, central to her problem with Canadian law, Elisabeth's *mother* tongue is inoperable in the courts of law, where only English is spoken (e.g., trans., 27; 39).

Woven in and out of Elisabeth's thought processes, which are focused primarily on guilt and betrayal, we note how she remembers scraps of her mother's opinions and teachings: e.g., "Mother doesn't believe in cards. Or in love either" (trans., 37); or, "And my mother says we have to find me a husband..." (trans., 61). In fact, Elisabeth is marked in the womb by her widowed mother's grief: "My mother, deep in mourning, carrying me in her womb. Like the stone inside the fruit...Poor little child, growing in a black crepe cocoon...Could I glimpse the world outside through the red, weeping eyes of this young widowed mother of mine?" (trans., 47). As the mother remains inconsolable, the aunts must take over the raising of the fatherless rebellious child. Elisabeth's mother is only one step removed from Stevens Brown's in *Les Fous...:* she along with her husband would leave her children in the forest to die, or drown them like kittens. Indeed, her unwanted twin daughters are turned over to their uncle, the Reverend Nicolas Junes for whom they become lifelong servants, even slaves.

Most particularly, Elisabeth's mother dreads telling her the "facts of life" when she sees she is about to marry Tassy: "Madame d'Aulnières bursts into tears. Dreads having to explain to her daughter the mysteries of marriage and death. For her, one and the same" (trans., 64). And again, as Elisabeth recalls how she prodded her mother to "tell her" or to give her advice, the mother's inadequate and dreamy teachings are remembered: "Is this how little girls grow up? I preen you and primp you, fix your hair. I send you off to mass and catechism. I shield you from life and death...We get babies from the Indians. They come by and drop them into women's beds...Love! Beautiful love of song and story" (trans., 65). The reader is made all too aware through many of Elisabeth's recollections of the mother's (and the aunts') failure to teach the young girl about the objective realities of life. Added to this, as

Elisabeth's first marriage disintegrates, her mother proclaims, "It's no good for a woman to stagnate in the country with her husband" (trans., 93); in her half-mad view, every married woman first gives birth to a daughter, and then becomes a widow as soon as she can! (trans., 93).

The most vivid recollection Elisabeth has of her relationship to her mother is the latter's presence at the first and second encounters with Dr. Nelson. Although by and large the mother has abdicated her nurturing role, leaving it to the pious and withered maiden-aunts, nonetheless when Elisabeth falls ill and the doctor must be called, her mother quite aggressively takes over: Elisabeth recalls repeatedly how her mother pulled the covers around her chin; how she put her to bed and tucked her in; how she stood at the head of the bed, in charge as it were (trans., 103; 104; 107; 108; 110). Clearly her mother is her lost paradise; she is recalled at this crucial moment as being for once the guardian, "stately and solemn, like an angel sculpted on a holy font..." (trans., 108).

Yet the mother, who had always been dysfunctional prior to those scenes in which Nelson is introduced to Elisabeth, disappears from the scene following her aggression in the face of Elisabeth's illness. After taking this tentative stand, and after attempting to cover up the source of Elisabeth's injured arm (trans., 110), she resumes her habitual lifelessness (trans., 159), falls to taking naps (trans., 139) and ultimately fades from the picture and dies (trans., 204-5).

Alas, then, the epiphany in which her mother would lovingly take over the care and protection of her daughter is short lived; and, more bitter still, it is bound to fail: soon after, as Elisabeth remembers it, "My mother goes back to having her headaches and shuts herself into her widowhood again. As if my fate has been sealed now for good" (trans., 111). It is this jansenistic fatality, the linchpin of Hébert's tragic vision throughout her oeuvre, that follows our heroine Elisabeth down the *cul de sac* of her terrible ordeal; all characters are included in its ring, so that the edenic bonds that would otherwise bless her life and those around her cannot be maximized. All this runs counter to the teachings of her Catholic religion; yet this is how she understands the events of her life, a "countryside unused."

Indeed, this formulation of her impotence in the face of her destiny and the loss of a functioning mother not only render Elisabeth abulic, but this view of her life also takes us back to our earlier meditation on the first garden as portrayed by Anne Hébert. For the first garden was inhabited by the first mother, who lost for all of us heaven on earth, through the first sin, original sin. And original sin is a major preoccupation of our author, who, as we have seen, has devoted two major poems to Eve, and returns again and again to that turning point in humanity's history, often by oblique reference. Truly, Hébert almost invariably sets her characters under that jansenistic "curse" of original sin and incapacitating fatalism. If anyone ever escaped it (doctrinally at least), it was the Virgin Mary, and one notes reference to that in *Les Enfants du sabbat,* in which, as noted earlier, the nuns belong to the fictional Order of the Immaculate Conception. Not so lucky Nora whom the pastor likens in her putative sinfulness to Eve. In reality, however, the pastor is the greater sinner. In reality the figure of Eve, primogenetrix, is enormously attractive to Anne Hébert. And in reality one can postulate that the problems revolving around the concept of original sin (emanating from the story of the first mother) --- as reflected in Anne Hébert's writings --- are frequently evoked ironically. It is quite likely we should conclude that for Hébert this is a "myth" of male fabrication, a device invented to blame woman for the fall and the subsequent expulsion from the first garden and its fruits. Note, for example, how, like the pastor of *Les Fous de Bassan*, Nelson in *Kamouraska* blames that "damned woman," and even indirectly likens her to Eve, when he says "Evil Elisabeth, all because of you..." (trans., 188). And this strategy is even more apparent in the case of Stevens Brown, who is arguably the sole narrative voice of the entire book *Les Fous...*[5] (just as Elisabeth is the sole voice of *Kamouraska*). Stevens Brown, a self-declared misogynist, a rapist and murderer, is in the process of disculpating himself, of repeatedly showing the desire of the two cousins, and of shifting blame throughout.

Nonetheless, the pervasive cloud of fatality hangs over all; human reason cannot prevail; madness sets in (trans., 193), and, as Elisabeth herself proclaims, "...beyond all saintliness the wily innocence of beasts and madmen reigns supreme" (trans., 171). The sentence has a rather Pascalian or Racinian ring.

Concluding Statement

A careful examination of Anne Hébert's writings will, then, support the thesis that the mother-daughter theme is all-engulfing; that archetypal grandmothers as well as aunts (e.g., Felicity in *Les Fous...*" the aunts in *Kamouraska*) are indeed mother figures who cast influence on the female (and often on the male) protagonists, and who remain energized even after their death in the psyches of their descendants. It should be noted that often the Jungian terrible mother figure is present in the "story" as is the case in *Les Fous de Bassan* (as seen through Felicity), and in *Kamouraska*, as is manifest through Elisabeth's ominous mother-in-law (Antoine's mother).

Added to this, these mothers and grandmothers join the ranks of the mothers of Greek myth, especially Demeter, and of the mothers of Judeo-Christian biblical accounts --- being identified in particular with Eve. As I have suggested, the relationships of sisters and cousins are implicated in these connections as well. Though one encounters the strong mother (grandmother) figure in many Québécois novels (*Maria Chapdelaine* of Louis Hémon; *Bonheur d'occasion* of Gabrielle Roy; *Une saison dans la vie d'Emmanuel* [A Season in the Life of Emmanuel] of Marie-Claire Blais: etc.), in the works of Anne Hébert these connections, these *fils conducteurs* (or connecting rods) are so intertwined and so complex (indeed at times so pathological) that they may well be called at once the source of order and of disorder in the personal lives of her characters and, as Hébert envisions it, in the borderless realms of the outer world as well. Ideally, such lines would lead back to the first garden, to an Eden, to the bliss of the womb or to perfect love, but in all cases it seems the characters are doomed not to find their way through the tangled mass of wires that their lives have become.

Works Cited and Bibliography

Hébert, Anne. *Les Enfants du sabbat.* Paris: Seuil, 1975. [*Children of the Black Sabbath]*. Translated by Carol Dunlop Hébert. Don Mills, Ontario: General Publishing Paperbacks, 1982.

______. *Dialogue sur la traduction. With Frank Scott. Introduction by Northrup Frye.* Montreal*: 1970* Editions HMH.

______. *Les Fous de Bassan.* Paris: Seuil 1982. [*In the Shadow of the Wind].* Translated by Sheila Fischman. Toronto: General Publishing Co. Ltd., 1982.

______. *Héloïse.* Paris: Seuil, 1980. [*Héloïse].* Translated by Sheila Fischman. Toronto: General Publishing Co. Ltd., 1983.

______. *Kamouraska.* Paris: Seuil, 1970. [*Kamouraska].* Translated by Clarence Gagnon. Toronto: General Publishing Co. Ltd., 1973.

______. *Le Jour n'a d'égal que la nuit* [*Day Has No Equal But Night*]. Translated by A. Poulin, Jr. Brockport, N.Y. : Boa Eds., Ltd., 1994. (French texts copyright by Boréal, Montreal, 1992.) (See also the bilingual Anne Hébert, *Selected Poems.* Translated by A. Poulin Jr., Brockport, N.Y. : Boa Eds., Ltd., 1987).

______. *Poèmes.* Paris: Seuil, 1960.

______. *Le Premier Jardin.* Paris: Seuil, 1988.

______. *Le Torrent.* Montreal: Beauchemin, 1950. Enlarged edition, Montreal: HMH, 1965.

Jones, Elizabeth. *Gentlemen and Jesuits.* Toronto: University of Toronto Press, 1986 (1991, paperback edition).

Maillet, Antonine. *Le Chemin Saint-Jacques.* Montreal: Leméac, 1996.

Mésavage, Ruth M. *L'Archéologie d'un mythe: Le Premier Jardin d'Anne Hébert.* Quebec Studies, 10, 1990: 69-78.

McPherson, Karen S. *Incriminations: Guilty Women/Telling Stories.* Princeton, N.J.: Princeton University Press, 1994.

Pallister, Janis L. *Eros and Thanatos in Anne Hébert and Marguerite Duras: Kamouraska and Hiroshima mon amour. Dalhousie French Studies* 10, spring, summer, 1986: 56-71.

______. *Orphic Elements in Anne Hébert's Héloïse. Quebec Studies*, 5, 1987: 125-134.

______. *Renaissance forebears of Anne Hébert's Enfants du Sabbat (nouer l'esguillette). Il tema della Fortuna.* Giudici Festschrift. Milan, Italy: 1990, 519-527.

______. *Satanism, Jansenism and Greek Myth in Anne Hébert's "Fous de Bassan." Carrefour de Cultures.* Edited by Régis Antoine. Gunter Narr Verlag (1993).

Randall, Marilyn. "Les Énigmes des *Fous de Bassan*: féminisme, narration et clôture." *Voix et Images* #43, Fall, 1989, 66-82.
Rich, Adrienne, et al. *Of Woman Born*. New York: Norton, 1986.
Slott, Kathryn. Review of Anne Hébert's *Le Premier Jardin*. *Quebec Studies* 9, 1989-1990, 161-163.

Additional Reading:

L'Autre Lecture: la critique au féminin et les textes québécois. Directed by Lori Saint-Martin. Montreal, Quebec: XYZ, 1992.
Contemporary Quebec Criticism. Edited and translated by Larry Shouldice. Toronto, Buffalo: University of Toronto Press, 1979.
Dionne, René. *Bibliographie de la critique de la littérature québécoise et canadienne-française dans les revues canadiennes.* Ottawa: Presses de l'Université d'Ottawa, 1986.
Erman, Michel. *Anthology of Quebec and French Canadian Literature.* Laval, Quebec: Editions Beauchemin Ltée. 1996.
Francophone Literatures of the New World. Edited with introduction by James P.Gilroy. Denver, Col: Dept. of Foreign Languages & Literatures, University of Denver, 21982 (Occasional Paper).
Jones, Elizabeth. *Gentlemen and Jesuits.* Toronto: University of Toronto Press, 1986 (1991, paperback edition). (The founding of Nouvelle France).
Littérature canadienne-française et québécoise: anthologie critique. Edited by Michel Erman. Preface by Paul Syczynski. Chomedey, Laval, Quebec: Editions Beauchemin, 1992.
Louder, Dean R. et Eric Waddell. *Du Continent perdu à l'archipel retrouvé: Le Quebec et l'Amérique française.* Quebec: Les Presses de l'Université Laval, 1983.
Mailhot, Laurent and Pierre Nepveu. *La Poésie québécoise des origines à nos jours. Anthologie.* Montreal: Les Presses de l'Université du Quebec; Les Editions de l'Hexagone, 1980.
Pallister, Janis L. *The Cinema of Quebec.* Cranbury, NJ: Associated University Presses, 1995.
Smith, Donald. *Voices of Deliverance: Interviews with Quebec & Acadian Writers.* Translated by Larry Shouldice. Toronto, Buffalo: Anansi, 1986.
Tellier, Sylvie. *Chronologie littéraire du Quebec: 1970 à 1960.* Quebec: Institut québécois de recherche sur la culture, 1982. Montreal: Presses de l'Université de Montréal, 1989.

Manuals:

Balthazar, Louis, *French Canadian Civilization*. ACSUS Paper. (Wash. DC) 1989.
Hamblet, Edwin. *La Littérature canadienne francophone.* Paris: Hatier, 1987.
Weiss, Jonathan. *French-Canadian Literature.* ACSUS Paper (Wash, DC), 1989.

On *Les Fous de Bassan:*

Marie-Dominique Boyce. "Création de la mère'mer: Symbole du paradis perdu dans *Les Fous de Bassan." The French Review* 68, 1994, 294-302.
Karen Gould. "Absence and Meaning in Anne Hébert's *Les Fous de Bassan." The French Review,* 1986, 921-30.
Leslie Harlin. "Unreliable views of the feminine in Anne Hébert's *Les Fous de Bassan." Quebec Studies* 21-22, 1996. Harlin: "No one wins in *Les Fous...* I see no triumphant matriarchy. The only female character who keeps her voice into infinity is doomed to forever roam the scene of her murder and will forever exist within her bad faith." Harlin further claims that patriarchy also dies. Unpatriarchal; loss of linear, grammatically correct styles of previous testimonials.
Marilyn Randall. "Les Enigmes de *Fous de Bassan:* Féminisme, narration et clôture." *Voix et Images* 15, 1989, 66-82.
Pallister, Janis L. *The Cinema of Quebec* (op. cit. supra, 184-209). For deep analysis of the book versus the film.
Slott, Kathryn. Expression, Obsession, and Re-emergence in Anne Hébert's *Les Fous de Bassan." American Review of Canadian Studies* 17, 1987, 297-307.

On *Kamouraska:*

Carbonneau, Alain. "Kamouraska, roman et film." *Revue d'Histoire Littéraire du Quebec et du Canada français 11,* Winter-Spring 1986, 93-100. "Far from being a copy too close to the novel, the film reworks the signs within its stripped down nature...; it thus operates a symbolizing appropriation. From scripting to projection a redistribution of the structures of the imagination is brought about." (My translation.)
Gingrass, Katharine. "Writing the Unconscious: Dreams and Reverie in Anne Hébert's *Kamouraska.*" *Quebec Studies* 12, Spring-Summer, 1991, 139-145.
Pallister, Janis L. *The Cinema of Quebec* (op.cit. supra). For deep analysis of the book versus the film.

Saint-Martin, Lori. "Ecriture et combat féministe: figures de la sorcière dans l'écriture des femmes au Quebec." *Quebec Studies* 12, Spring/Summer, 1991, 67-82. Discussion of La Corriveau; also of some works by Anne Hébert (*Les Enfants du Sabbat,* Aurélie in *Kamouraska*); Jovette Marchessault --- and others.

Endnotes

[1] All the important mythological figures referred to in this essay are explained below:

Adonis was a Phoenecian god whose cult reached Greece and Alexandria, where his legend evokes the cycle of vegetation. Killed in the hunt, Adonis sojourns a part of the year with Persephone, in the Kingdom of the dead, and each sprintime he returns to Aphrodite, among the living.

Artemis was the Greek goddess of Nature and the Hunt. She is armed with bow and arrow, is accompanied by dogs that were a gift from Pan, and lives in the mountains or woods. Inviolable and unviolated, she expresses her anger at virgins who give in to love, and she makes priestesses of those who refuse. The Romans knew her by the name Diana.

Demeter was the Greek goddess of cultivated land. Her daughter Persephone (Core; Cora) having been abducted by Hades, the weeping Demeter traveled over the earth looking for her, until Zeus ordered the god of the Underworld (Hades) to restore the daughter to her mother six months out of the year. Her principal cult was at Eleusis.

Medusa was a denizen of the sea, ruler and queen, whose staring eyes could terrorize, and the glimpse of whom could turn one to stone. Perseus cut off her head --- while averting her glance ---; ultimately, her ghost dwelt in Hades, where it terrified the dead.

Persephone was the daughter of Demeter, also called Core, or "maiden." She was carried off by Hades to the Underworld. When Demeter, mad with grief, ceased to make the land fertile, Zeus asked Hades to let Persephone return to her mother for a part of the year. Persephone was venerated by the Romans under the name Proserpina.

Phedra, or Phèdre in the Racinian play that Flora is in, was a heroine of Greek mythology. She was the daughter of Minos and Pasiphae, sister of Ariadne, and wife of Theseus. Enamored of her stepson Hippolytus, who resisted her advances, she accused him of having tried to violate her. Once Hippolytus was executed, she hanged herself. Her passion inspired Sophocles, Euripides and Racine, among others.

Telemachus was a hero in Greek mythology of the Trojan cycle. The son of Odysseus and Penelope, he was still a child when his father departed for the siege of Troy, and his education was confided to Mentor. At a given point he left home in search of his father who was long in returning from the war. He helped his father fight against pretenders and to recuperate the throne of Ithaca.

[2.] See bibliography for articles in which I have already explored various aspects of the mother-daughter relationship and the mythic elements in Hébert. Additionally, these articles are built around the concept of Eros locked in battle with Thanatos, a Hébertian theme not to be overlooked in any of her works --- any more than that of original sin. This would include *Le Premier Jardin*, where self-love struggles with self-extinction, or self-erasure, as an important variation of the Eros-Thanatos dyad.

[3.] Kathryn Slott's recent presentation at ACQS on the "discours transatlantique" in the Hébertian novel can have considerable bearing on this.

[4.] This is the contention, at least, of Marilyn Randall in "Les Énigmes des *Fous de Bassan*: féminisme, narration et clôture." *Voix et Images* No.43 (Fall 1989): 66-82.

[5.] Incidentally, Radi, heroine of Antonine Maillet's most recent book, *Le Chemin Saint-Jacques*, pictures the very womb of her mother as Eden, or *le paradis* (perdu) [paradise (lost)]; and this lost Paradise is, by extension, a metonymy of Acadie. Antonine Maillet. *Le Chemin Saint-Jacques*. Montreal: Leméac, 1996.

Jacques Poulin

Ritt Deitz
University of Wisconsin, Madison

One of Quebec's most critically acclaimed living novelists, Jacques Poulin has produced a body of work that speaks as much to the question of Francophone identity in North America as to the place of the individual within that identity. Poulin's eight novels (to date) span four decades and reflect a number of significant transitions in Quebec fiction, many of which are linked to important societal changes, such as the breakdown of the family and the increasing presence of technology in French Canada in recent years. Yet Poulin's work is not polemical or political. His novels tend more to reveal such realities subtly, through stories that are personal, playful, and real.

Born in 1937, in Saint-Gédéon-de-Beauce, Poulin obtained his *licence en orientation professionnelle* in 1960, at the Université Laval. In 1964, he received another Laval *licence* (graduate degree), this time in letters. Subsequent positions in counseling and translation, work Poulin did in Quebec City between 1967 and 1973, seem to have nurtured the nascent writer's dual penchant for language and psychology. It was in this period that Poulin wrote his first three novels: *Mon cheval pour un royaume,* (1967) [*My Kingdom for a Horse*]; *Jimmy,* (1969); and *Le Cœur de la baleine bleue,*(1970) [*The Heart of the Blue Whale*] (translated together in 1979, by Sheila Fischman, as *The "Jimmy" Trilogy*). As noted in the *Oxford Companion to Canadian Literature,* these novels (all three written in the first person) steer clear of the standard themes of their times in Quebec fiction: namely, "the Church, the land (escaping from it or rediscovering it), Quebec's political affairs" (Toye 675). Instead, they reveal a personalized Quebec, as seen from behind unique sets of eyes --- those, respectively, of a terrorist, an eleven year-old boy, and a heart transplant recipient. All these stories unfold in and around Quebec City (usually in *le Vieux-Québec*, the oldest and most historic part of the city), which inextricably links psychology and narrative with *geography*. In these novels, the meaning narrators make of their lives is usually bound up in some way with the various meanings of Quebec City and the province itself.

The upheaval of Quebec's "quiet revolution" is somewhat visible in Poulin's early work. For example, Pierre, the protagonist of *Mon cheval pour un royaume,* is confined to a psychiatric ward for his part in the bombing of a historic monument. Yet although the act is political and the locale is Quebec City (the provincial capital and symbolic center of francophone Canada), Pierre's foremost characteristic is that he is a *writer.* Not only is he a writer, but one whose intellectual activity often distances him from the lives of others. For Ben-Z. Shek, Pierre's participation in the bombing is "a symbolic way of breaking out of his shell" (122), although not far enough to prevent his mistress, Nathalie, from having an affair with a mutual friend, a carriage driver named Simon.

From his very first literary effort, then, Poulin has placed the writer at the center of his fiction, together with such intimate realities as friendship, erotic love, and self-inquiry. In this novel and the two that follow, the political and historical realities of life in Quebec serve mostly as a background for personal drama. (Larger issues of language and culture do not really surface until Poulin's 1984 novel, *Volkswagen Blues,* where they vie neck-and-neck with the subjective concerns of that novel's protagonist.)

Heavily influenced by the work of J.D. Salinger, Poulin's second novel, *Jimmy*, is narrated by a boy who lives in Cap Rouge, with his writer father and emotionally unstable mother, in an old riverside cottage held up only precariously by rotting pilings. The father spends days drinking Molsons in his attic study, where he works on a book about Hemingway, one of Poulin's most oft-mentioned literary favorites; the boy's mother has been unable to recover fully from the loss of a child. Jimmy spends his days weaving in and out of this harsh reality, which he softens with imaginative play and conversations about race cars and riverboat piloting. It is difficult to decipher the blurred line between Jimmy's inner world and what is *really* happening, since the narrator is the boy himself. Yet certain themes are instantly apparent: the writer, suffering in some way and isolated from the rest of society and his own loved ones; the alienated, narrating protagonist; the vast and irrevocable power of the Saint Lawrence, over both the land and the writer's imagination.

In Poulin's third novel, *Le Cœur de la baleine bleue,* the major themes from the first two works return, creating a continuity: Noël, the novel's narrator, is a writer and recovering heart-transplant patient who spends the whole story coming to terms with his new, more fragile existence. His wife leaves him for a hockey star named Bill, a man of action and physical health, with an English name. In short, Bill is the exact opposite of the frail, bookish narrator whose post-operation days consist mostly of exploring the "pôle intérieur" [the internal pole] of his existence. Noël's retreat into himself is characterized by hallucinatory visits from Charlotte, the adolescent donor whose heart beats in Noël's chest. He calls her "Charlie, the blue whale", hence the book's title, because of the color of her veins and the rhythm of her pulse, which vaguely reminds him of a whale's. In his waking life, he spends much time gazing out of windows at the Saint Lawrence, one of Poulin's thematic touchstones. In such passages, Noël's fate seems as inevitable as the tides, and as linked to the outward flow of the water as Quebec City is to the river itself.

Noël's serious medical condition confines him to his neighborhood. As narrator, he refers to his story as an "histoire de cœur" ([a love story] and, literally, a "heart story") between himself and *le Vieux-Québec*. Replete with descriptions of actual streets, restaurants, cafés, bookstores and the like, parts of this novel read like a nighttime stroll. Yet the reality residing behind each location is that of Noël himself, a totally unique character, one who, at once, knows the city like the back of his hand, avoids the American tourists who "depersonalize" the true charm of the city, and realizes the fragility of his own life within this place with which he is, in all senses of the word, in love.

These first three literary efforts reveal a number of important things about Quebec writing of the period, and about Poulin's own place in its canon. Alongside the recurrent themes they contain --- the conflict between writing and living, the fragility of erotic and familial love, the streets and waters of *le Vieux-Québec* --- these books announce what will become a major characteristic of Quebec life throughout the 1970s, both in the novel and in social and political life there. The "quiet revolution" begun in the 1960s continued to wrest power, both literally and figuratively, from the Catholic Church and all its ancillary institutions (bourgeois marriage, anti-syndicalist sentiment, and so on); but by the early 1970s, life in Quebec had taken a decidedly inward turn, toward a national identity based on exclusion from Canada itself. Quebec fiction already reflects this turn in the work of writers like Jacques Godbout, whose heroes, according to Maurice Cagnon, become aware of their "identity within a 'French Canadian' society that is in the process of becoming a 'Quebec' society" (74). Generally speaking, many scholars of Canadian studies locate the beginning of this trend in the "October Crisis" of 1970, in which Prime Minister Pierre Trudeau imprisoned thousands of Québécois (most of them in Montreal) suspected of involvement in the terrorist FLQ (Quebec Liberation Front). Trudeau's "heavy-handed implementation of the War Measures Act" flew in the face of Canadians' assumed civil liberties, according to critics of the crackdown, since those targeted were arrested without charge and denied access to legal consultation (Ayres). Ben-Z. Shek interprets the event's impact on the novel in the following way:

> The decade at first did not mark a sharp break with the preceding one, in which the politicization of the novel was an important trend. As it went on, however, there was a certain inward-turning by many writers, with more concern for the micro --- rather than the macro --- society (100).

Certainly, Poulin's first three novels *already* consitute an "inward turn" in many ways, especially since they focus on the anxieties and joys of personal experience. If the major themes of Poulin's work are indeed "the quest for tenderness, the daily process of death, and the conflict between creativity and responsibility" (Saint Pierre 310), then it is surely in these first three novels that they echo with the greatest force. Around these individual stories, Poulin weaves a quite believable contemporary Quebec, built on details of life there in the late 1960s: actual hockey players and sports figures, streets and cafés, brand names. Yet what most strongly characterizes these novels is the uniqueness of the *individual lives* that Poulin asks us to imagine. Again, Poulin's "major and continuous preoccupation" with writing, his "subtle and muted tonality," his "simple and classical style," and his "timid sexuality" (Shek 121) all force contemporary political reality into a translucent background. Yet as the effects of events like the October Crisis begin to surface in Quebec's literature, Poulin himself moves on to other territory, having already prefigured the major literary exploration of Quebec's interior landscapes, both physical and psychological.

In a sense, Poulin's two 1970s novels, *Faites de beaux rêves* (1974) [Sweet Dreams] and *Les Grandes Marées* (1978) [*Spring Tides*], constitute an even further withdrawal from the contemporary political realities of the decade in Quebec, even more so than his already very "inward" first three efforts. *Faites de beaux rêves* is the story of a group of friends and revolves around a car race, resembling the narrative subjectivity of *Jimmy,* but with three identifiable points of view. *Les Grandes Marées* is the story of Teddy, a comic-strip translator, whose editor sends him to live on an island in the Saint Lawrence, where he spends his time working and playing tennis with an automated serve-and-volley machine. In these novels, Poulin is arguably at his most experimental. This is especially true of *Les Grandes Marées,* which is composed of both standard, narrative text and alternative kinds of writing and images, such as menus, traffic signs and drawings.[1]

Likewise, Poulin's habit of numbering and titling chapters draws the reader's attention to this book's narrative experiments. For instance, following a lengthy group discussion about literature and "marginal types" in society, there is a one-sentence chapter, entitled "Un heureux événement" [A Blessed Event]:

> Un heureux événement se produisit dans la cabane de Marie: la chatte mit au monde trois petits chats, deux noir et blanc et un tout noir (174). [A blessed event occurred in Marie's cabin: the black cat gave birth to three kittens, two black-and-white and one all black.][2]

In the very next chapter, "Les questions pertinentes" [Pertinent Questions], the translator and his companion Marie discuss "all the cats they'd ever had in their lives," after which "Marie posa une série de questions" [Marie asked a series of questions]. "She didn't usually do this," says the narrator, who immediately disappears behind a question-and-answer, scripted dialogue:

> Q: Qu'est-ce que tu vas faire?
> R: J'en sais rien.
> Q: Ton travail, c'était important pour toi?
> R: C'est ce que je pensais... Maintenant, j'en suis moins sûr (175).
>
> [Q: What are you going to do?
> R: I have no idea.
> Q: Was your work important to you?

R: I thought so... but now, I'm not so sure] (*Spring Tides* 145).

The dialogue goes on for another twenty-six "lines" then shifts back to the dominant, third-person narrative. It opens up once more, however, to quote the full text of the warning label atop Teddy's Coleman stove.

In Poulin's first three novels, the personal dramas that define the stories are nonetheless strongly associated with the place in which they unfurl. The characters always seem to have an aesthetic appreciation for, or some kind of visceral connection to, the details: of the Château Frontenac, the cafés, the tides, and such. While this is true to an extent in *Les Grandes Marées,* the region serves as little more than a setting with which Poulin is familiar. Ultimately, the novel's greatest feature is its innovative form, its "exploration of the possibilities and the limits of narration" (Toye 676).[3]

There are small hints at social critique in these two books. For instance, Saint Pierre and Smith interpret the tennis machine in *Les Grandes Marées* as a gesture whereby Poulin aims to "expose technology as dangerous, seeing technology as a phenomenon that isolates and alienates mankind" (310). Yet such interpretations seem a little strong when one considers, say, Poulin's unadulterated love of cars, boats and the Volkswagen minibus, a love that permeates his whole body of work. In any case, the role of machines (and technology in general) is dwarfed by the unabashedly self-conscious narrative form of these novels. This is especially true of *Les Grandes Marées,* the novel that surely constitutes Poulin's most adventurous foray thus far into the plasticity of literary language.

The next big political milestone for Quebec was the 1980 referendum on sovereignty and association, in which Quebec separatism was again defeated at the polls there. This event, according to Ben-Z. Shek and others, marked an end to the inward-turned literature of the 1970s. The event coincided with (and perhaps influenced, at least partially) Quebec writers' "expansion of the spatial contours of the novel to the wide world" (Shek 125). A major part of this geographic expansion in the themes and subjects of Quebec fiction was the relatively sudden, broad-based inclusion of the United States, a phenomenon "termed *américanité,* or America consciousness" (125).

Although Shek associates the beginning of "America consciousness" with the 1980 referendum, *américanité* itself is only partially political. It is a phenomenon that has begun to permeate the fabric of daily life in Quebec, on most every level, especially in the marketplace. Ralph Saronak characterizes this period as concurrent with the decline of an older Quebec society, whose cultural boundaries were as much defined by its Catholicism as by anything, say, on television or in stores:

> Quebec is a consumer world by the early 1980s, a *pays* where tinsel and the tacky blue paint of Catholic kitsch have been displaced, although not yet entirely replaced, by gadgets and overheated malls stuffed with piles of tight-fitting designer jeans *fabriqués aux Etats-Unis* (19).

The infiltration of Quebec's material culture, as described by Saronak, is of course only part of the equation. Broadly speaking, *américanité* has as much to do with the Québécois sense of space as it does the vicissitudes of the marketplace. Marshall McLuhan characterizes the entire, dominant North American sense of space as grouped around "two psychic poles... the outer space for aggressive extroversion and the inner space for cozy sociability and security amid dangers" (McLuhan 231). The product of North American civilization's "nineteenth-century war on the empty wilderness," this sense of space is unique not only to Québécois, but to all Canadian and American mentalities, according to McLuhan (230). It is for these reasons, and others, that Poulin's 1984 novel *Volkswagen Blues* places him at the top of the most oft-cited literary witnesses of Québécois *américanité.*

The novel chronicles a few weeks in the life of a middle-aged Québécois novelist named "Jack Waterman,"[4] who drives his Volkswagen minibus across North America in the company of a young *métisse* hitchhiker called "Big Grasshopper." At first, the object of his journey is his older brother Théo, missing for several years but who has sent Jack a postcard bearing only the facsimile of a text by Jacques Cartier, with no return address. Jack and Big Grasshopper attempt to track Théo by researching textual clues that lead to others, spending much of their time in obscure libraries and at sites where the often competing histories of French, English and Indian North America are played out. Such conflicts occur even between the travelers, an aging white man and a young, half-Montagnaise woman, who nonetheless agree that, both as a *place* and a *story*, America is built on centuries of blood and violence.

Having spent much time frequenting writers and artists associated with the Beat movement, Théo finally turns up in San Francisco, near the end of the novel. Paralyzed by "creeping paralysis" and in the company of a social worker, however, he is unable to recognize his own brother and cannot even understand his native language. "I don't know you" is all he can say to Jack.[5] At the end of the novel, Jack gives his bus to Big Grasshopper, who has decided to stay a while in San Francisco. Having discovered a lot of things, few of which he actually expected, Jack has decided to fly home and resume his life as a novelist, in Quebec City.

Several aspects of this novel are noteworthy: one is the broad and fundamental question of Francophone identity on a continent dominated by the English language. *Volkswagen Blues* is the first Poulin novel to attack this question in a direct and systematic way. That Jack Waterman is a writer enhances one's awareness of the language he must use: everywhere he travels, west of Quebec province, he must use English to get the information he needs to find his brother. (Finding one's way to a lost brother is, at least partially, a quest for a tangible fragment of one's own intimate past, and there is certainly irony in Théo's total loss of his mother tongue. Is this a metaphoric warning to Quebec readers about the hand-in-hand power of English *and* culture in the United States?) One of the most necessary travel accessories in the bus is Jack's dictionary, his "inner space" is made secure, in part, because it is a *French-language space.* In the vast spaces of the Midwestern and Western United States, Jack and Big Grasshopper rarely encounter others who can speak French. In McLuhan's terms, every time they leave the bus they are cast adrift, in a wilderness of language. Even though they can understand it, the English language nonetheless remains outside the Québécois sense of home.[6]

Another characteristic of this novel is its attention, albeit rather superficial, to issues of ethnicity: *Volkswagen Blues* also constitutes *américanité* in its hashing out of American Indian identity, between Big Grasshopper and Jack, but also in the young woman's own ambivalence about her mixed heritage. "Who am I?" is the question implicit in every page and, practically, every sentence, not only for characters, but for the groups they represent (including those with which the reader identifies) and the places themselves.

Volkswagen Blues is also an homage to American literature, especially to the Beat Generation in general, and to Jack Kerouac in particular, whose *On the Road* is an explicit influence on Jack Waterman and on the novel itself. Novelist Saul Bellow is an actual character in the story, as is the poet Lawrence Ferlinghetti. Still other Beat poets figure in the novel, in a photo supposedly showing a young Théo. (Like *Les Grandes Marées, Volkswagen Blues* experiments with alternative kinds of text, but the prose itself is a fairly straightforward, third-person narrative.) Broadly speaking, this is Poulin's most "outward" novel to date. In many ways, it is less coherent than earlier work, Poulin tries to cover a great number of large questions in a novel that becomes, in some ways, a literary equivalent of *National Geographic.* Yet its ambitious reach, beyond the confines of a homebound quest for Québécois identity, is a remarkable example of *américanité.* For that reason, it should remain interesting for a long time, to many North American readers, for as many reasons as a reader can find in its pages.

By the late 1980s, Poulin seems ready to return to an "inward" kind of writing, but this time in a more mature and polished way. In his 1989 novel, *Le Vieux Chagrin* [*Mr. Blue*], he returns to a number of his favorite themes, among them tenderness, mortality, desire and imagination. It is the story of Jim, a professional novelist who lives alone with his cat ("Chagrin," or Sorrow), in the house in which he was raised on the Saint Lawrence. He lives primarily by daily rituals: making and drinking coffee, reading, playing tennis, writing (or trying to write), eating, going for walks on the banks of the river. Into this metered and sparse existence enter three main characters or groups: Jim's brother, with whom he plays tennis; the mysterious "Marie K.," whose sailboat and personal effects occupy an inlet and small cave and who never once actually meets Jim; and a group of women who live in a shelter/collective in Quebec City, one of whom eventually becomes a sort of surrogate daughter to the lonely writer.

Jim feels he is in love with the elusive "Marika," whose copy of the *Thousand and One Nights* he periodically studies in the cave she occupies. While he leaves her notes, builds a special mailbox for their correspondence, and even sends his brother to meet her, she never once appears to him or even responds to his letters. What appear, instead, are pages describing the spaces he must cross to find her: vast panoramas of sand, rock and tide, bordered on one side by the inlet and cave and, on the other, his decrepit old house, decaying symbolically on the hill overlooking the wide water.

Jim's own personal relationship with this landscape bears a certain resemblance to the one linking Jimmy to the river, in Poulin's first novel. One recalls the family's ritual, springtime inspection of the pilings in *Jimmy*, when the boy, his parents, and a neighbor slosh through the mud around the pilings that support the house. Jimmy explains the procedure:

> On discute toute l'affaire: il faut que tu examines les dégâts causés par les grandes marées de l'automne précédent et les glaces de l'hiver, et que tu décides si les pilotis peuvent tenir le coup une autre année (32).
>
> [We talk about the whole business: you have to see what damage has been caused by the high autumn tides and the winter ice, and then you have to decide if the pilings can make it through another year.][7]

Here, as in other scenes in *Jimmy,* the point at which water meets land inevitably conjures absence and loss. In this case, it is the precise place in which his family's unraveling is played out, and where, eventually, the pilings will break loose entirely. Yet glances across vast expanses of water are also an important thread in the psychology of characters' relationships in *Jimmy,* as in a scene where Jimmy's parents reminisce about a ferry ride they have taken together as a young couple. Marie remembers asking Papou, during this ride, if he could see "the lighthouse at Sainte-Pétronille on the Ile d'Orléans." He did not answer. "I was fascinated," he responds, "the ferry was headed straight for the lighthouse you were pointing to" (The "Jimmy" Trilogy 79). Poulin places many similar, sweeping gazes across the water in *Le Vieux Chagrin,* as in this scene, where Jim considers Marika's apparent hiding place from atop a rock on the banks:

> [L]a main en visière à cause des reflets du soleil sur le fleuve, j'examinai systématiquement les rochers du rivage, puis la grève qui au loin se courbait comme une épaule, et même la falaise plantée de pins, mais il n'y avait pas âme qui vive. Il fallait attendre encore (50).
>
> [Shielding my eyes from the sun, because of its reflection on the river, I systematically examined the rocks on the bank, then the beach, which,

> in the distance, curved around like a shoulder, and even the cliff, all covered with pines. But there wasn't a soul to be found. I would have to wait some more.]

In *Le Vieux Chagrin,* Jim's use of the landscape is rich and metaphoric. As a character, he dwells on the edge of land and water, in a decaying relic of his own childhood. His inspections of this land-and-waterscape all relate to his general well-being, in particular, to his quest for whom he senses will be his ideal female partner. Characters in *Jimmy* relate similarly to their place at the water: they understand it as both an indication of their ability to communicate with one another and a barometer of what the future will bring them in their life there.

The natural setting in *Le Vieux Chagrin* also serves as a kind of symbolic bridge between Quebec City (whence comes the group of women, periodically, to visit with Jim and fix his leaky roof) and a purely natural North America with which all Québécois may identify. Throughout French-Canadian and Québécois literature, according to Jack Warwick, there has been a recurrent attempt to connect, thematically, the wilderness of the far north and French civilization in the cities of the Saint Lawrence valley. One of the results of this "tendency," he writes, "has been the creation of a land of illusion which has all the epic qualities of the North, without being too far away from civilization." Such a realm, which Warwick calls a "near North," is also very practical with regard to individual identity in the novel: this "near North" often serves to frame a "dramatic contrast between man in society and man confronting a wider cosmos" (41). While the wilderness "frame" here is more *water* than woods, Jim's own existence at the edge of the river nonetheless incarnates both kinds of relationships, as Warwick defines them, in *Le Grand Chagrin.* It is at the same time a book about a writer's ongoing work and, at a more profound level, a middle-aged man's aging body and waning chances for love.

As I have already discussed to some degree, the individual Québécois's relationship to the place he occupies pervades and defines Poulin's fiction from beginning to end. Poulin's most recent novel, *La Tournée d'automne* (1993) [Fall Tour] is no exception. Opening at the Terrasse Dufferin, in the heart of *le Vieux-Québec,* the story moves in a great loop, up into the "near North" of the upper Saint Lawrence, then back to Quebec City. The protagonist, a middle-aged man known simply as the Chauffeur, drives a "bookmobile" to tiny towns up and down both banks of the river, dispensing any and all literature both to small groups of regular patrons and to anyone he meets along the way who appears interested in reading. A number of aspects of this last novel are significant, and they all in some way serve as a kind of synthesis of Poulin's entire body of work to date.[8]

First, there is the Frenchwoman whom the Chauffeur meets and falls in love with, and whose travels loosely follow his own. Called Marie, she physically resembles the Chauffeur, both in age and physiognomy (her thin face and hollow cheeks recall the female double of Poulin's previous novel, also named "Marie"). The Marie of *La Tournée d'automne* incarnates Poulin's ongoing fascination with intimate male-female duos, particularly those in which the male character sees himself, to some degree, in his female counterpart. Yet Marie also permits Poulin to treat the difficulties of both male and female aging as never before. Not only is the Chauffeur's attraction to her tempered by his fears of declining health; he also drops hints, to Marie, about eventually choosing suicide over the slow fade of aging. One concrete detail that Poulin keeps between the Chauffeur and the reader is the length of rubber tubing that the latter keeps in his bus, tubing long enough, ominously, to reach from the tailpipe to the driver's-side window. (*Volkswagen Blues* is also full of anxiety about male aging, yet with two major differences: first, while Jack Waterman is in his forties, his traveling companion, Big Grasshopper, is barely in her twenties; and second, Jack's concerns about growing old figure among other, equally important themes, such as literature and the writing of American history. Aging and the possibility of suicide in *La Tournée d'automne* constitute the closest thing to suspense one can find in all of Poulin.)[9]

Besides his preoccupation with old age and death, the bulk of the Chauffeur's existence appears in smaller acts, peppered here and there with broader and more poetic statements but which remain, mostly, accounts of what he drinks, wears, and says as he drives the bookmobile across vast stretches of the near North. Like most Poulin heroes before him, the Chauffeur has a fondness for coffee, hot chocolate and corn flakes. As Ginette Michaud has noted, he is strikingly similar to Jack Waterman in his culinary tastes, his speaking style, and the way in which he warms his sleeping bag (3). His daily routines are also filled with cats, who --- as in most of Poulin's other novels --- appear in his path at every kind of moment. Like most of Poulin's heroes, the Chauffeur finds both solace and despair, moment by moment, in the details that make up his days.

Exactly how Poulin's work will fit into the Quebec literary canon in future years is, of course, a mystery. Yet any examination of his work, ostensibly still in progress, ought at some point to imagine possible answers, since what his novels "mean" can be, roughly speaking, as diverse and contradictory as the cultural fate of Quebec itself. Invariably, his novels portray characters at the edge of a new existence, rapidly unfolding: life without family, new hope for love, a second life in one's native city, the sadness and release of death. In this sense, he keeps company with writerly contemporaries like Marie-Claire Blais and Réjean Ducharme, whose characters are usually "poverty-stricken" and "acutely conscious of being insufficiently loved" (Cagnon 112). Yet Poulin's work also draws him into a circle of Québécois novelists interested in writing and the language of fiction *as subject matter:* Hubert Aquin, for instance, whom Cagnon finds "preoccupied with textual processes as such and their autonomous artistic functioning" (98), or Victor-Lévy Beaulieu, whose books often highlight both the writing process and certain characters who "reappear in book after book" (122). In any case, as a storyteller, Poulin's forays into the human condition have an unusually broad appeal, even in translation, especially to readers from European and North American cultures.

Nonetheless, fluctuating in cataclysms that coincide with Poulin's career, Quebec's interest *in its own cultural identity* lives and breathes across his eight novels, and should, if his fans are lucky, continue to do so. Readers interested in Poulin as a specifically Québécois writer have a special question to ask as we ponder where he will take us next: what will happen to Poulinian fiction in the years following Québec's October 1995 referendum on sovereignty, in which the separatist vote came closer than ever to winning some form of national autonomy for the province? And more interestingly perhaps, what turns may we now expect from the Quebec novel as a whole?

Works Cited and Bibliography

Ayres, Jeffrey. Letter to the author. 3 December 1996.

Cagnon, Maurice. *The French Novel of Quebec.* Boston: Twayne Publishers, 1986.

Leland, Marine. "Quebec Literature in Its American Context." David Staines, Editor. *The Canadian Imagination: Dimensions of a Literary Culture.* Cambridge, MA: Harvard University Press, 1977, 188-225.

McLuhan, Marshall. "Canada: The Borderline Case." David Staines, Editor *The Canadian Imagination: Dimensions of a Literary Culture.* Cambridge, MA: Harvard University Press, 1977, 226-48.

Michaud, Ginette. "Sur la route (bis)," *Spirale* 130 (février 1994), 3-6.

Poulin, Jacques. *Le Cœur de la baleine bleue.* Montreal: Editions du jour, 1970.

_____. *Faites de beaux rêves.* Montreal: Leméac, 1974.

_____. *Les Grandes Marées.* Montreal: Leméac, 1978.

_____. *Jimmy.* Montreal: Editions du jour, 1969.

_____. *The "Jimmy" Trilogy.* Translated by Sheila Fischman. Toronto: Anansi, 1979.

_____. *Mon cheval pour un royaume.* Montreal: Editions du jour, 1967.

_____. *Mr. Blue.* Translated by Sheila Fischman. Montreal: Véhicule Press, 1993. Translation of *Le Vieux Chagrin.*

_____. *Spring Tides.* Translated by Sheila Fischman. Toronto: Anansi, 1986.

_____. *La Tournée d'automne.* Montreal: Leméac, 1993.

_____. *Le Vieux Chagrin.* Montreal and Arles: Leméac/Actes Sud, 1989.

_____. *Volkswagen Blues.* Montreal: Editions Québec/Amérique, 1984.

_____. *Volkswagen Blues* Translated by Sheila Fischman. Toronto: McClelland and Stewart, 1988.

Ripley, Gordon, and Anne Mercer, Editors. *Who's Who in Canadian Literature.* Toronto: Reference Press, 1985.

Saint Pierre, Paul Matthew, and Donald Smith. "Jacques Poulin." *Dictionary of Literary Biography, vol. 60: Canadian Writers Since 1960, Second Series.* Detroit: Gale Research Co., 1987.

Saronak, Ralph. "Accentuating the Differences." *Yale French Studies* 65 (1983), 3-20.

Shek, Ben-Z. *French-Canadian and Québécois Novels.* Toronto: Oxford University Press, 1991.

Toye, William, Editor *The Oxford Companion to Canadian Literature.* Toronto: Oxford University Press, 1983.

Warwick, Jack. *The Long Journey: Literary Themes of French Canada.* Toronto: University of Toronto Press, 1968.

Weiss, Jonathan. "Une lecture américaine de *Volkswagen Blues*." *Etudes françaises* 21(1985-86), 89-96.

Additional Reading:

Purdy, Anthony. *A Certain Difficulty of Being: Essay on the Quebec Novel.* Montreal: McGill-Queens University Press, 1990.

Handler, Richard. *Nationalism and the Politics of Culture in Quebec.* (New Directions in Anthropological Writing.) Madison: University of Wisconsin Press, 1988.

Endnotes

1. An aggressive quoter of both European and North American novels, Poulin shows a particular affection for American writers, especially Ernest Hemingway, in all his novels. Critics have also noted such authors' influence on his style, as in *Jimmy's* simarity to the stories of J. D. Salinger. In *Les Grandes Marées,* William Toye sees two other American literary influences: Richard Brautigan and Kurt Vonnegut (Toye 675).

2. Spring Tides 144.

3. Similarly, Matthew Saint Pierre and Donald Smith see *Les Grandes Marées* as a novel that, mainly, puts forth "the central aesthetic question of whether fiction is in essence mimetic or nonmimetic"(310).

4. Readers of Poulin notice the recurrence of similar names in his novels, names which usually have some similarity to "Jacques." In *Le Vieux Chagrin* (1989), the lone writer is named Jim; a secondary character in *La Tournée d'automne* (1993), a writer who drives a Volkswagen minibus, is named Jack. Critics have long noted Poulin's fascination with notions of symbiosis and "doubles" (characters, personalities that resemble and seem made to complement each other); his character names have an autobiographical feel that seems, in a way, an extension of his fascination with duality. (See Michaud 3-6.)

5. The sentence is in English in the original French-language edition. So are many other of the novel's dialogues, in which the travelers talk with museum staff members, national park guides, and even the novelist Saul Bellow, who tells Jack, "You can speak French if you want: I was born in Montreal" (109).

6. Even the U.S.-Canadian border itself, between *anglophone* Ontario and Michigan, hints at this alienation. Jonathan Weiss argues that, as Jack and Big Grasshopper contemplate the crossing, the border "sépare la vie de la mort, la voix du silence" ("separates life from death, the voice from silence," Weiss 89). While this is true to some extent in *Volkswagen Blues,* the greatest separation is surely between spaces defined by French (Quebec and the bus) and English (practically everywhere else).

7. The "Jimmy" Trilogy 76.

8. Poulin recycles part of earlier work from the very beginning of the novel. In the first paragraph, the Chauffeur leans out the window of his apartment, which

is on the fifth floor, and gazes onto the city and parts of the river. As it is described, the Chauffeur's apartment is practically interchangeable with Noël's in *Le Cœur de la baleine bleue.*

9. Yet the way that the reader *learns* of the rubber tubing recalls the dual concerns about aging and no longer being able to write, anxieties one finds in most of Poulin's books. As one of the Chauffeur's clients asks specifically for an *unpublished manuscript*, he must choose between two boxes. One contains such manuscripts, the unrecognized fruit of difficult literary labor; the other contains tools and the piece of tubing (*La Tournée d'automne* 75).

Progress and Its Paradoxes: Dreaming the Machine in the Québécois Novel[1]

Jean-François Chassay
Université du Québec à Montréal
Translated from the French
by Éric de Larochellière

For the average man --- including numerous science technocrats --- scientific language must be regarded as neutral and unambiguous. It serves to objectify facts from which knowledge has been continuously transformed since time immemorial with the object of improving the condition of humanity. This naïve and simplistic view disregards the complexity of the social field and isolates science from it, as though rhetorical and institutional factors could not affect science. However, in these fin-de-siècle years, even scientists --- among others --- have called the idea of stable and universal values into question.[2] For a long time --- even now, for that matter --- many scientists have been inclined to set themselves up as "keepers of the truth," forgetting that their own truths are essentially relative and conditional. Without falling into the trap of absolute relativism (the worst defect of what is called, for lack of a better term, postmodernism), it would be naïve to disregard the social environment which allows for the arrival of the new. It must always be remembered that scientific texts are precisely that: *texts*, marked by polysemy and metaphor, inseparable from the discursive background in which they originated, and it is also necessary to consider that, in other respects, science contains a significant proportion of fancy, of imagination, on which, among other things, culture depends, literature even more so.

These preliminary remarks serve to indicate the angle from which I would like to approach the Québécois novel. My text will consist of a (necessarily) brief diachronic survey in which I will examine the impact of scientific and technological innovation on narrative fiction. More machine; this phenomenon has become all the more striking with the passage of time, for "the everyday artifacts of technoscience are easier and easier to operate (while) their conception is more and more incomprehensible."[3]

The word "machine" being vague, and its definition allowing a wide range of meanings, I will limit myself here to three functions of the machine: to compensate for the individual's deficiencies with regard to speed (transport), information (telecommunications, media), and cognition (computers, automata). In other words, I will question the role assigned to machines, which have become natural extensions of human beings in western societies, and which allow them to *accelerate* their knowledge of the world. Although transport will be considered, the machines in question will mainly consist of those subordinate, but integral, to the new communication networks and functioning in part on a virtual level. Moreover, the texts I will be discussing (mostly contemporary) are in keeping with the epistemological pattern of the postindustrial era (or rather, of postmodernism).

When fully represented in a text, such machines do not only perform a thematic role --- they appear at one and the same time as a fantasy (of ideal or nightmarish society), as body in motion (around, and because of, which society is transformed, distorted and re-formed) and as knowledge (the machine impresses its mark on the world, compelling us to rethink the outlines of our reality).

As we know, the emergence of literature in Quebec is recent. Although there were texts published as far back as the seventeenth and eighteenth centuries (whose status as "Canadian" texts is often problematic, for that matter), the first novel is published in 1837, and moreover literary institutions develop only in the late 1890's. At the end of the nineteenth century, *L'École littéraire de Montréal* (the Literary School of Montreal), however significant its mark on Quebec's literary history, consists mostly of notaries and lawyers interested in (the technical aspects of) language above all, and in the eyes of whom publishing a collection of poems serves only to make their curriculum appear "tasteful". Furthermore, because the Canadian Francophone population is increasing only moderately, the number of publications in French remain limited. In this context, the study of Québécois literature, from the angle which interests me here, is intriguing on account of its singular position, both historically and geographically: in the nineteenth century, Québécois literature tentatively emerges, and it does so in a subjugated and marginalized society, very much uncertain of its identity. The most interesting aspect of the connection between science/technology and Quebec's literature can be summarized in two words, particularly significant: foundation (of the country, of new myths, etc.) and north-Americanness.[4]

The exogenous development of industry in French Canada in the mid-nineteenth century, as well as the relatively minor place given to science in Canada's Francophone centers, place Québécois literature in an ideological and discursive context particularly fruitful for studying the *introduction* of science and technology in literature. In addition, the numerous ambiguities surrounding the idea of progress in French Canada render the ideological background confusing. The relations between Quebec's population and that of the United States have always been complex and ambivalent: land of progress, home of scientific inventors (especially of "communicating" machines) --- the neighboring country has an influence on the various attempts at modernization in Quebec which appear, as the case may be, in a favorable or unfavorable light.

It is in this particular setting that the machine is represented in the texts of Québécois writers, as early as the nineteenth century (notably through the role played by transport). From an ideological point of view, the train will play an important role in the relations between Quebec and the United States, as seen in Honoré Beaugrand's novel *Jeanne la fileuse* (1879) [Jeanne, the Spinner]. In this work, which chronicles the vicissitudes of French Canadians who have emigrated to New England, the importance of the train is due to its ambiguous role in the text: it is the reason for the rapid increase of emigration, but also the way (or one of the ways) which permits the reversal of the trend, going back home.

Beaugrand lived and worked in the United States as a journalist; he wished to restore the reputation of Francophone emigrants inhabiting the towns of New England. Opposed to emigration, he attacks Quebec's politicians nonetheless, because they refuse to see the real cause of these departures en masse. Contrary to what is believed in Quebec, says Beaugrand, French Canadian emigrants do not live in a state of extreme poverty; his goal is to demonstrate this throughout his novel.

After her father's death, and when her brother and her fiancé have gone to work in the north, Jeanne Girard desperately looks for a job. By accident, she knocks at the door of a family whose generosity and kindness are equal to their recent destitution, resulting from the disastrous state of the economy. Welcomed as if she were one of the family, Jeanne moves with the couple and their six children to Fall River, where she becomes a spinner, and eventually the local heroine, thanks to her goodness, her modesty and devotion to work.

A conservative love story, needlessly complicated by simplistic political reflections, *Jeanne la fileuse* is nonetheless valuable as a document, because it explicitly links Quebec to the United States, by means of the train, the symbol of progress *par excellence*.

The train can also be seen as a sign of a new Romanticism --- the crossing of great landscapes constantly changing, at a speed never reached before, allowing the individual to confront the world in a way previously unthinkable --- and as a sign, in this period of positivism, of the new powers of science and technology. As Christophe Studeny writes,

> By itself, it symbolizes the dynamism of an era, the inexorable acceleration of contemporary time: indeed what could pride itself better than the railroad on an intimate harmony, on a perfect affinity with the western nineteenth century? Because of its mode of propulsion, its components and its fuel --- the famous triad of vapor-metal-coal --- the technical engineering which results in its rapid improvement, the systematic extension of the ramifications of its network, because of the hourly discipline, the meticulous accuracy it imposes, [...] finally because of the decompartmentalization of a world riveted to the ground, it seems in its movement to bring the century along with it.[5]

The idea of progress in a general way is what the train is all about, not only the progress of technology. As Leo Marx notes: "In the popular culture of the (nineteenth century) the railroad was a favorite emblem of progress --- not merely technological progress, but the overall progress of the race."[6] This power, in Beaugrand's novel, is manifested in the relations between French Canada and the United States. What is, in Beaugrand's opinion, one of the major problems of Canada's previous governments? The refusal to "facilitate the opening of new thoroughfares, to the detriment of the country's agricultural and commercial interests" (230). And still --- the comparison is unavoidable --- the example of the United States is there to demonstrate that the "creation of railroads, of roads and waterways was the key to transforming the wild America into a rich and prosperous country, in less than a century" (230). From this statement, we can gather that the train is a symbol of Americans' interest in communications; it reads implicitly as a sign of a progressive nation, whereas Canadians seem retrograde, and even reactionary.

Therefore, it is for good reason, and with full knowledge of the situation, that the Francophones of Quebec leave for the United States: the thoroughfares, owing to trains and to the quality of the railroad network, allow one to go to a country where the belief in progress accounts for the nation's wealth and industrial development.

This justification for Canadians' self-imposed exile cannot erase the fact that emigration impacts negatively on the country. Nonetheless, the train potentially permits the resolution of the dilemma, as shown by the celebration of Midsummer Day, June 24, 1874. That year, the Saint-Jean-Baptiste Society sent a letter of invitation to all national societies in the United States, a fervent appeal to the emigrated Canadians' patriotism, encouraging them to take part in the national festival in Montreal. Not only does the swiftness of the train allow a speedy return to their native country, but the proliferation of railroad companies allows a healthy *(sic)* capitalist competition making the rates decrease drastically, thereby prompting greater numbers of emigrants to come back.

In this way, paradoxically, the train both makes exile easier and encourages people to return. Its existence, to quote Beaugrand once again, gives rise to "a new facility in establishing relations between citizens of different countries" (229). Thus, there really is a link between Quebec and the United States: it is exile no more, but rather the spreading of the "family".

This power of the train, which makes it the symbol of the nineteenth century according to Studeny, gives it a mythic dimension. In Pierre Chauveau's *Charles Guérin* (1853), the narrator likens man to the locomotive:

> The swift, blazing locomotive, flying from one mountain to another, running quick as lightning over precipices, crushing everything which

stands in its way, is no more pitiless than the man who wants to make his way in the world (93).

At the beginning of the following century, *Robert Lozé* (1903), a novel by Errol Bouchette, opens with a scene in which a couple of young workers silently admire what is then the largest bridge in the world --- the Victoria Bridge. And a train is the first thing they see: "All of a sudden, Cyclops out of a chasm, the locomotive rushes along the shore, pierces the air with its whistle, then, like a meteor, hauling its long tail of coaches, passes by and disappears in the night" (3).

This collision between technology and mythology fascinates the two young people: "Near the dark arch (they) have stopped and remain still, a graceful group which stands out against the black background of this frame. Except for the faraway roaring of the rapids, all the noises have ceased" (4).

The fact that the idea of progress predominates in these two novels where the train gains a hyperbolic dimension is significant. Pierre Guérin "wish(es he) was the leader of progress" (48) while Bouchette's novel glorifies the techno-industrial development; the protagonists dream of seeing in Quebec the same thing that is happening in the United States. The presence of the train in both novels connotes the *acceleration of speed*, a notion well-suited to the idea of progress, and which arises simultaneous to the rapid growth of technology, from the beginning of the nineteenth century until contemporary times, a continuation of the works which allowed the diffusion of electricity. The expansion of high-speed transport --- in which we can see the paradigm of energy and the metaphor of motor --- reads as a phenomenon bound up with progress. It goes without saying that opposing progress leads, as a necessary corollary, to a refusal of modern transport, which is considered to be an abominable manifestation of the contemporary world, contrary to the "true values" of a Catholic.

The conservative, if not reactionary, ideology in the novels of the early twentieth century is expressed as fear and at times irrational dread of modern transport. In Harry Bernard's *Dolorès* (1932), a lawyer leaves Montreal for the Laurention region to investigate a murder case. Disgusted with the effects of tourism --- "leprosy rotting nature and landscape" (32) --- he notices that the lakes are "filled with Jews on holiday" (30; *sic.*). This world is marked by "the railroad, black and stinking" (55) and by automobiles falling into disrepair:

> Man's hand has stamped its mark everywhere. Asphalt roads. They crawl in the valleys, skirt peaks, cling to hillsides, or they set out straight to conquer the heights, like at the *côte du Sauvage*. The cars run away, wheeled fireballs. Screamings of horns, gasoline and oil odors, grindings of gears carelessly shifted (29-30).

In that world, where a dubious purity is searched for, even the radio announcer's voice, with "the coldness of a February snow" (93), is held up to public obloquy. The racism, insidious or obvious, which is found in numerous novels of that time signifies an implicit fear: the multiplicity of the means of transport --- their increased speed and convenience --- leads inevitably to an opening of the continental space, to a simplification of movement, facilitating exchanges between "races".

Cars, these machines with "their deafening purr", as Adolphe Brassard describes it in *Péché d'orgueil* (1935) [Sin of Pride], are the cause of multiple crashes, an allegory of progress which, basically, precipitates catastrophes.[7] This is exactly what Siraf (the ghostly eponymous "character" of the 1934 novel *Siraf* by Georges Bugnet), declares appearing from who-knows-where, foretelling the coming apocalypse to the narrator, an apocalypse which will be caused by human inventions:

> Men, women, children, poisoned by your tinned foods scientifically prepared, torn to pieces by your automobiles, crushed by your locomotives, beheaded by your aeroplanes, roasted in your airships, smothered by your gasses, butchered by your surgeons, shredded by your explosives (20).

We could not think of a more spectacular --- or more ridiculous --- way to illustrate the belief that production of contemporary machines is contrary to the human spirit.

It is no wonder that these conservative, ideologically simplistic novels are no less simplistic from a literary point of view. Essentially didactic, grounded in propaganda and Manichaeism, they make narrative use of the machine to stress an already self-evident message.

The development of the Québécois novel in the last decades has brought about much richer results. The fast growth of telecommunication systems and the consumer society explosion, as well as the increasingly pervasive presence of the media, form the backdrop against which the novelistic narration often develops:

> With the advent of the fluid paradigm,[8] what has fractured is the image of a power located in a single point of the society, conspicuous and univocal, the image of a central power thoroughly connected with the periphery. What is taking shape is the image of complex networks of places whose very muddling up makes decision-making complex. With this complexity must correspond the multiplicity of interpreting instruments.[9]

Numerous novels account for this complexity. Between the airplane and the computer, the telephone and the televisual image, the boundaries often become confused: the "nonlinearity" of communication networks gives evidence of a new way of looking at the space-time framework, indissociable from a new way of perceiving reality. We are now entering, in the words of French essayist Régis Debray, the "medialogy" period (*l'ère de la médiologie*), which should allow for the integration of a history of broadcasting revolutions with the history of transport revolutions.[10] So important is this new reality, especially among the publications of the past two decades, that I will merely give a few examples which seem to me particularly significant.

From the perspective of this text, the publication, in 1954, of *Alexandre Chenevert* by Gabrielle Roy may be regarded as an important point in the development of the Québécois novel. Beneath the psychological story --- on the whole, rather banal --- of a bank clerk appears the impact of modern communications on the mentality of urban man. The novel accounts for the ways in which information circulates in the urban environment, and shows how an individual trying to obtain information can be touched, changed, even alienated by the forms through which information spreads. Newspapers, radio, publicity bombard him with news which he is unable to process.

Harry Bernard's novel evoked the coldness of the radio announcer's voice, but it is with greater subtlety that Gabrielle Roy sees the urban world; she represents it as a media-saturated world where the discursive and social fabric tends to homogenize individuals and to make them similar to the "faceless voice" which speaks on the radio at the beginning of the novel, interrupting Chenevert's train of thought, chanting, "the world has become one and indivisible" (11). Does not

Alexandre, when his boss finishes talking to him, notice that he reproduced "the tone of most speeches on the radio"? (285).

For the majority of the novel's individuals, their response to the open-ended and polymorphic world in which they live, the entropic delirium of information, can be reduced to this lowest common denominator: in the face of complexity, most people --- especially Monsieur Fontaine, Chenevert's boss --- take refuge behind a language which merely reacts automatically, according to the dictates of the ideological and economic system in which they live, the social discourse to which everyone is inclined to refer.

Alexandre Chenevert, on the other hand, is overwhelmed not only with the multitude of contradictory information --- which reaches him from the four corners of the world --- that he cannot assimilate, but also with the power of marketing, which interferes constantly with political discourse and distorts it, treating it as if it was no more than a new product to be launched. Within this context, the very notion of value becomes difficult to categorize, causing the discursive shifts beginning with marketing and proceeding as far as issues of geopolitical balance: "Take an aspirin. Aspirin spells: A-S-P-I-R-I-N. Buy a Lux bar of soap. Germany must be destroyed. Germany must be rebuilt. It foams" (23).

The relevance of Gabrielle Roy's novel is due to its insight into mental processes --- the mental processes of people in the urban media environment following World War II (whose effects we are only now beginning to see and understand). Alexandre Chenevert is a character who has not yet been able to invent *his own language* and is capable only of repeating information exactly as he hears it. Overwhelmed by the manifestations of urban information, he feels incapable of asserting critical positions from a subjective standpoint. But he is a perfect example of the difficulty experienced by a naïve mind (spontaneous, sincere, and natural in the original sense of 'naïve') trying to differentiate between propaganda, publicity and something approaching genuinely objective information. It is even possible to say that the novel tends to demonstrate the impossibility of this objectivity.

Twenty years later, in a completely different manner, Réjean Ducharme also tackles, in *L'Hiver de force* (1973) [Winter of Force] the power of media discourse which envelops the individual, creating a world where silence is no longer possible. Not only do the various media multiply information, making it difficult to understand the world, but the individual himself is called to account, as the narrator André Ferron affirms, in his own way:

> A thousand masses moving, armed with mikes, with typos, with photos, with labs, fight over our humble opinion, and to defend ourselves we have only the methods of mediocre loners, unhealthy and dirty: curses, gossip, tricks [...] For we definitely want to own ourselves, on our own, and keep what we have (that is so fleeting that it has gone or changed as soon as we think that we touched, saw, named it), most obviously our hatred for everything that makes us *want*, as if *dispossessed* (13-14).

This refusal to be manipulated by media accounts for a level of awareness which Alexandre Chenevert did not have, but which immerses the two protagonists in paranoia. One of the major differences between Gabrielle Roy's novel and Réjean Ducharme's is the result of the unavoidable presence of the television, whose discourse is similar to the discourse of the people encountered by André and Nicole Ferron.

In *Le Roman à l'imparfait* [Novel in the Imperfect], Gilles Marcotte wrote that the Ferrons "experience the world just as television represents it, as a promise and a disappointment; they experience it to the point of absurdity. For them, *everything is TV.*"[11] In fact, if there is a convergence between reality and television, it is because the latter distills little more than absurdity. Moreover, the movies that the Ferrons watch on the small screen are never considered works of art, food for thought permitting the development of a critical mind. They even confess their disappointment when the scheduled movies are too "interesting": "Katharine Hepburn, Jeanne Moreau, Sophia Loren... Personally we find masterpieces trashy and it's great actors we can't stand" (103).

Reality is experienced like a movie: either Nicole and André project themselves into the televised film ("Now we're in Venice. It's Sangrido Bembo and Eleonora Remi's wedding day" [51]) or the television follows them:

> We're out of the restaurant, but not of the shameless exploitation of which we've been the victim. With the result that over and above what we want to vomit but are unable to, snatches of dialogue from *Comment qu'elle est* rush to our throats:
> — *Do you know Venice?* asks Eddie Constantine.

— *No, we've never been introduced!* answers Françoise Brion (37).

But their reality crosses the screen, when for example they see their friend Petit Pois ("La Toune") repeating for television viewers "what she had whispered (to them) as if it was a shameful drama" (76). Moreover, the narration is always interrupted by what is said on the screen: the Ferrons are worried that Petit Pois will call while they are watching a horror movie; they are sad because she did not call at the agreed time, just when the local hockey team loses a game in the playoffs, etc.

Between the movies which André and Nicole watch, the telephone whose ringing they desperately await, the radio which serves as background noise and the stereo (on which they play records that are soon after thrown out), among all that is said and shown, nothing is worth remembering or thinking about. Worse, everything which is experienced resembles a recording.

Everything is reduced to the television screen and to what can be quickly consumed; the language becomes empty of authenticity. When a taxi driver explains his daily routine (123-124), the scene is narrated like a report. The character seems "real" but out of context, without any connection with what occurs before and what comes after, his account loses all interest, besides sounding lifeless. This information does not leave any impression on us.

There always seems to be a discrepancy between what happens and what individuals say. Nicole and André do not deal with human beings, but rather with "characters" who behave as if they were on television, addressing thousands of viewers; after the receipt of a telegram from Petit Pois, André Ferron writes: "We kind of feel that it's a poem and that it's not aimed at us, but at all of humanity" (156). The people whom they meet are fashionable. Therefore, they will not last. They are big news, they are part of current events, but they are empty and spineless. Images with no depth, they participate in changes and will disappear with them.

Furthermore, the language which they use is the (urban) spoken language heard on the radio, on television, in commercials. "The very notion of history, like that of war, of contradiction or of tragedy, implied the primacy of the printed word and the accumulation of time corresponding to it. These inventions go back as far as the *graphosphère*."[12] In *L'Hiver de force*, we preserve little and write even less—and we write so badly! The Ferrons, who are meticulous copy editors, realize this with every new contract.

Their friend, nicknamed either Petit Pois or La Toune, perfectly represents the individual born of and for the "videosphere,"[13] inclined to what we could call a "self-communication": "By constantly speaking well of her love, she had ended up feeling love for her love. She desired herself, with juicy eyes" (44).

L'Hiver de force's pathetic paradox is due to the fact that, in the novel's media environment, the tragic is not possible anymore; it is transformed into "curses, gossip, tricks" (14). In order for tragedy to appear, duration is necessary. But this *accelerated* world forbids it. Words are slogans and slogans are ridiculous.

"There is a study to be done," writes Régis Debray, "[...] on the relations between the evanescence of traces and the disillusionment of the world. Between the lightening of supports and their symbolic sinking."[14] From this point of view, *L'Hiver de force* provides a spectacular example of the world's disillusionment in the era of contemporary technology. "The *tendency to the weakening* of traces cannot not strike the observer. It is manifested historically as the increasing ephemerality of supports, which seem to have a shorter and shorter lifespan: the flip side of --- and the price of --- a larger and larger diffusion."[15]

Deeply critical, Ducharme's novel gives the image a presence within the text, so that image and text collide in a dialectical process, the image creating the social discourse as the latter is being transformed by the former.

The "information machine" (such as television, but also computers) and the "transport machine" seem to become increasingly connected. Once more, as Régis Debray explains, the contemporary period is propitious to a "medialogical" analysis:

> There is an actual solidarity between the electric telegraph and the railroad, the radio and the airplane, the television and the rocket. A chronological and cultural relation. Since there are historical atlases, we could imagine medialogical atlases, reconstructing the worlds, the geographies constructed by each communications system, and we would maybe see how the time required for travel and transmission

simultaneously modifies the space --- at once imaginary and real, fantasized and operative --- of humans.[16]

In this context, it is no surprise that some novels bring together the fastest information system (the computer) and the fastest transportation system (the airplane). Both are symbols of speed, and summon virtuality into the heart of reality. *Occupation double* (1990) [Double Occupation], a novel entirely structured by the presence of computers --- the first line introduces the protagonist, "J.B.S. Holdane, (a) software and microprocessor promoter at Ogivar technologies" (9)--- takes place mostly in airport waiting rooms. Here is a typically contemporary closed environment, a kind of "locked-room" setting, where the confinement paradoxically occurs in a place of holiday rush, a no-man's-land which calls for movement and instability. In this world where even a bookseller is named Bit (!), the computer has become the model of contemporary thought, in which the very idea of stability seems extravagant.

Similarly, *Programmeurs à gages* (1986) [Hired Programmers], can be interpreted as a reflection on the human condition in the era of computer science, when issues of information, and its processing, become central to the development of social structures.

Alain Bourque, consultant, works for a small American company which specializes in the protection of computer systems. A contract brings him to Montreal, where he will be working for Monnaies Transit International, which handles vast amounts of money, the transactions being entirely processed by computer. Following a leak, the company fears that their computer system has been infiltrated. Bourque is sent to find the error in the system, if it exists, and to identify the mole, if there is one.

Over and above the stakes of computer science and information transmission in the contemporary world, what is at stake above all is a new attitude towards mind and environment. In this context, Alain Bourque appears as the emblem of a social world in rapid, constant evolution.

In this respect, *Programmeurs à gages* seems to be a novelistic expression of Zbigniew Brzezinski's belief that we have entered the "technotronic society," a "society whose shape is culturally, psychologically, socially and economically determined by the influence of technology and electronics --- especially in the computer and communication field."[17] Therefore, North America gives the impression of being a network of large Americanized cities: Los Angeles, Boston, New York, Dallas, and Montreal are signposts, turntables whereby information can spread and circulate. Intermediate spaces do not exist anymore and temporality is shattered.

Symptomatically, Alain Bourque sees his boss unexpectedly turn up in the lobby of his hotel, while the reader still believes him to be in Los Angeles. People similarly appear and disappear throughout the novel, showing up suddenly when the need arises, as if distances are now meaningless. The surrounding environment is no longer the tangible, empirical world, which not long ago constituted the social world with which the individual could identify. For the North American, the surrounding environment, such as represented in *Programmeurs à gages*, is embodied by the airports and modes of transmitting information. As Paul Virilio writes:

> Urban planning is drifting, architecture is constantly moving around, the residence is merely the anamorphosis of a threshold. Despite those nostalgic for History, Rome is no longer in Rome, architecture is no longer in architecture, but rather in geometry --- in the space-time of vectors --- the esthetics of framework lurks among the special effects of communication machines, conversion or transmission machines [...] After the architecture-sculpture, it is the era of cinematographic artificiality, both literally and figuratively --- from now on, *architecture, it's all an act*; [...] the city is no longer a theater (an agora, a forum) *but the cinema of city lights* [...].[18]

Our sense of duration has changed, transformed by the atrophy of space. Clear distinctions, boundaries between things, as those dividing the inside from the outside, become confused. Working in the office of Monnaies Transit International, often in the "machine room," Alain Bourque sometimes looks as if he was conceived by the apparatus surrounding him. Thanks to (or because of) computer technology, the relations between individuals become apparent through the exploration of mediating machines, by the coding and decoding of information transmitted by more and more sophisticated technologies.

> The modification of the usual notions of time and space has extended the relativity principle to the ancient notion of *surface*, resulting in its replacement by the notion of *interface*, an underrated notion which

> nevertheless establishes the surface as it functions in media, and which changes it into a 'face-to-face,' a 'vis-à-vis.'[19]

The world surrounding the individual is a filter which acts on the consciousness. This new epistemological context can only lead to a crisis of the subject, the consequences of which are difficult to anticipate, especially as regards the subject's identity and sense of belonging.

But matters get complicated insofar as Alain Bourque seems to be truly enjoying this situation, which relates to his work. Proceeding with the investigation amounts to taking part in the treacheries and "hacking" which are everywhere in the North American communication network. His profession, as he says, is like a "a game of *Space Invaders*" (202). The contemporary world becomes an electronic labyrinth and Theseus is no longer the same.

This crisis of the subject caused by modern technology is present in other novels, such as those of Monique LaRue, Jacques Poulin or Pierre Billion.

Copies conformes (1989) [*True Copies*] by Monique LaRue, is set in California. Claire Dubé --- the narrator --- has come to San Francisco with her husband, a researcher in the field of artificial intelligence and machine language, who is working on a translation software project. Because he must hastily return to Montreal to see his mother, who has had a serious operation, he asks his wife to go to his office and pick up an important disk (the equivalent of sixty diskettes) which contains his past six months' work. But his desk is empty, and Claire finds herself reluctantly involved in a case of hacking.

The feeling of strangeness which haunts Claire, plunged into an unfathomable California, is significantly enhanced by the varied influence of technology. As her anguish grows, she seems trapped ever more tightly in the web of technology.

However, from an epistemological point of view, what plays an important role in the novel (on the level of both plot and narrative structure) are the reflections on computer science. The translation software on which Claire's husband was working induces us to question notions of copyright and value in the world of hypertext and "hyperreality," where one might have the impression that a good copy is worth more than the original. What does "being" mean in a world where everything seems to be leading towards artificiality? Throughout *Copies conformes*, the two meanings of the word "memory" are continually, implicitly opposed: the memory of the machine, objectified by automatic devices, detached from the body of individuals and from collective practices; and the memory of human beings, subjective, which at the same time allows them to re-create constantly their history and to have landmarks in their life, in the form of values derived from experience.

The clash between the individual and the machine is played out differently in *Les Grandes Marées* (1978) [*Spring Tides*], a novel which is based as much on the quest as on the inquest, like *Copies conformes*. This quest, in Jacques Poulin's novel, is above all a quest for an impossible solitude.

A man nicknamed Teddy Bear, a translator of comic strips for a newspaper, is asked by his boss what would make him happy. Teddy answers him by asking whether he has a desert island. And in fact, he does have one... Thus, Teddy will isolate himself in this place and work there, his boss coming once a week by helicopter to pick up the translations.

Little by little, the protagonist's world will be flooded by various people, who will occupy more and more space on the island, and thereby restrict Teddy's space. Furthermore, he will learn that his translations are never published. Ill, and less respected than those on the fringes of society --- being "outside the fringes" (198) --- he will finally throw himself into the water to escape the island and its population.

Even if he truly wants to isolate himself, Teddy nonetheless keeps in touch with consumer society, and even with techno-culture. The robot with which he plays tennis, the "Prince," is emblematic of this connection.

Regulated by an electronic brain allowing for a propulsion system equipped with an oscillator and a capacity of 125 balls, the Prince is certainly impressive. But its fascination goes beyond its technical properties: we could say that the technological object fascinates, in a tautological way, because it is technological. Marie, Teddy's friend, is impressed even before she sees it function. Its mechanical potential incites contemplation and fascination. The Prince appears as an archetypal representation of contemporary consumer society --- he who possesses such goods gains power from the simple fact that he has the means to dazzle his fellow men (Marie will say: "I like tennis very much as well, and I think that the Prince is very beautiful. She furtively caressed the translator's cheek [...]" [34]).

This mediating effect of the machine, operating here as a tool of seduction, accounts for the surprising blend of mythologies and new technologies in this novel: on the one hand, the tribal nature of the island, where there is a wish to leave things as they are, an interest in flora and fauna in a paradisiacal environment; on the other, a place where technology intrudes constantly --- an electronic robot for playing tennis, a teleprinter, a radio set for communicating with the boss of the newspaper, etc.

The signs of this telescoping of mythology and technology are obvious in the very first pages, when Teddy is seen working at his desk, in the office of the daily newspaper *Le Soleil*, a setting which implies, in the contemporary world, numerous modern technologies, particularly telecommunications and computers. However, nature is at hand: "the translator's desk was (standing) in the middle of a large room divided into islands of greenery by an arrangement of exotic plants and movable walls" (13). This kitsch reproduction of a natural world in the middle of a high-tech information center confirms that contemporary technology cannot exist apart from nature, the opposite being equally true.

The originality of *Les Grandes Marées* lies in its ecological interpretation of our world in these fin-de-siècle years. Isolation seems less and less possible in a world dominated by self-regulating systems; computer science is an artifact of occidental culture which we can no longer escape, since it permeates and shapes our everyday life: computers become the very model of our social functioning. As a result, we are perhaps the first civilization (or the first for a long time, at least in this form) to recognize that we live in an *ecological* world. Not in the trivial sense of the word, where it refers to protecting nature, but in the sense that we live in an ecosystem, a systemic world constituted of functional structures which, on each level of organisation, work towards the finality of the whole. Each element participates in the finality of the organism, and in return, the maintenance of the whole structure ensures the finality of each element.

In contemporary consciousness, this has contributed to the realization that if erosion affects the ecosystem, then it affects each one of the organisms which make up the ecosystem. In an insular world like the one in *Les Grandes Marées*, we witness a sort of suffocation of the island, due to a gradual invasion: in fact, we are witnessing an *ecological crisis*, a malfunctioning of the island's ecological system.

Jacques Poulin's novel, a model of today`s world, tends to show that we cannot escape our culture. Computers foreground a complex world of languages and programming, and also assert that, from now on, logic and a certain form of rationality are irrevocably part of the signs among which we live; we live in a high-tech world, an environment of objects, messages, codes, languages, evolving and changing by means of modalities which have very little to do with emotions. Moreover, this process supposedly takes place to the detriment of traditional values, rooted in humanism, of which Teddy is the last representative.

A good example of this objectification of the world appears in the last pages of the novel, when we learn that Teddy has worked in vain. Every week, he continues his gruelling intellectual work (we see him "think," constantly working, wondering about the meaning of words, revising his translations, etc.), to finally learn that it is actually a machine that has translated, in two minutes, the same comic strips that have been brought to him each week. The ultimate irony is that the computer is named "Atan," which means "man."

However, the novel avoids any moralism or didacticism, and in this rests its strength. If humanist values (through Teddy) appear to be crushed, it is mostly because they seem inadaptable. Teddy Bear is withdrawn and refuses to change --- or rather, cannot even think about changing. He is a self-contained man, rather rigid in his beliefs, and we could consider that, in this eco-technological context, his rigidity amounts to a *refusal of any form of otherness* (alterity), which is not necessarily a virtue.

We have seen the subject called into question by the computer in *Copies conformes*, and the ecosystem rethought through technology in *Les Grandes Marées*. *L'Enfant du cinquième Nord* (1982) [Child of Fifth North] by Pierre Billion tells, by means of the fantastic, the story of a young boy, a unique "biological machine," who notably has a strange power to disrupt computers.

Daniel Lecoultre, a high-ranking official in Ottawa, learns that his little daughter Florence has cancer. On the same floor of the Memorial hospital where the little girl is treated, Lecoultre notes the presence of a child with an odd stare, Max Sieber, kept strictly apart from the other patients. A rare disease? A virus? The mystery surrounding him continues to deepen. Gradually, though mostly by chance, Florence's father learns little by little that the boy has a curious talent for destroying, without even being aware of it, inorganic objects (especially any electronic apparatus which allows one to communicate and to orient oneself). And he might also have the power to save living organisms struck down by serious diseases.

Within the structure of a classic psychological novel (used most intelligently), Pierre Billion's novel explores, through the places where research is done (hospital, laboratory), issues related to bio-ethics as much as to genetics, to computer science as much as to physics. "The specificity of the biological, the genesis of the notion of information, the notions of structure and order are today at the center of a renewal of knowledge which has for its subject the world on a human scale."[20] From this point of view, the term "machine" must be understood here in a broad sense, incorporating the genetic machine that is the living body.

It is in a peripheral manner that the computer reveals its presence in this novel. The panic caused by the dysfunction of the computer system leads to a general contemplation on the very act of thinking, on cognition and related issues. Somewhere between myth and reason, *L'Enfant du cinquième Nord* investigates the idea of *open science*, in the words of Prigogine and Stengers, questioning the goals --- avowed and unavowed --- of scientific rationale and research.

From Louis-Philippe Hébert's *La Manufacture de machines* [The Manufacture of Machines] to Robert Racine's *Le Mal de Vienne* [The Sickness of Vienne], by way of Nicole Brossard's *French kiss*, we can find many novels in which science, and, in particular, the machines it generates, alters our perception of reality. Nevertheless, the few examples examined in the previous pages give, I think, a good idea, though fragmentary, of the possibilities opened by research which approaches literary texts from the perspective of science. The place occupied by the machine in literature allows us to question social discourse from a unique standpoint. The machine, as defined at the beginning of the essay, permits us to point out and to question the ideologies of the text, and to unravel the "discursive knots" which become apparent at some periods of history. The machine indicates, through the novel, the porous nature of the boundaries between the scientific, the philosophical, the sociological and the fictive. Novelistic prose accounts for gradual transformations of the machine, which cause at the same time various interrelated effects: ecological (the social environment is transformed), epistemological (the foundations of reality are modified) and literary (our language, our way of representing the world, is of course changed by our new perception of reality). This is a new field of exploration only recently pioneered by literary criticism; it has already proven extremely fertile.

Works Cited and Bibliography

Beaugrand, Honoré. *Jeanne la fileuse.* Montreal: Fides, 1980 (1879).
Bernard, Harry. *Dolorès.* Montreal: Albert Lévesque, 1932.
Billon, Pierre. *L'Enfant du cinquième Nord.* Paris: Seuil, 1982.
Bissonnette, Jacques. *Programmeurs à gages.* Montreal: VLB.
Bouchette, Errol. *Robert Lozé.* Montreal: Pigeon, 1903.
Brassard, Adolphe. *Péché d'orgueil.* Montréal: Imprimerie des sourds-muets, 1935.
Breton, Philippe and Serge Proulx. *L'Idéologie de la communication.* Montreal/Paris: Boréal/La Découverte 1989.
Bugnet, Georges. *Siraf.* Montreal: Éditions du Totem, 1934.
Chauveau, Pierre-Joseph-Olivier. *Charles Guérin.* Montreal: Fides, 1978.
Debray, Régis. *Cours de médiologie générale.* Paris: Gallimard, 1991.
_____. *Vie et mort de l'image: une histoire de l'image en occident* (Paris: Gallimard, 1992).
Désaulniers, Lucie. *Occupation double.* Montreal: Tryptique, 1990.
Ducharme, Réjean. *L'Hiver de force.* Paris: Gallimard, 1973.
Feyerabend, Paul. *Dialogues sur la connaissance.* Paris: Seuil, 1996.
Gobeil, Pierre. *Dessins et cartes du territoire.* L'Hexagone 1993.
LaRue, Monique. *Copies conformes.* Paris: Denoël, 1989.
_____. *Les Faux Fuyants.* Québec/Amérique 1982.
Latour, Bruno. *La Science en action.* Paris: La Découverte, 1989.
Lévy-Leblond's Jean-Marc. *L'Esprit de sel.* Paris: Fayard, "Points", 1984 [1981]
Marcotte, Gilles. *Le Roman à l'imparfait.* Montreal: La Presse, 1976.
_____. *Ibid.* 1976, 89.
Marx, Leo. *The Machine in the Garden.* New York: Oxford University Press 1964, 27.
Mattelart, Armand. *La Communication-monde.* Paris: La Découverte, 1991
Mattelart, Armand and Michèle Mattelart. *Penser les médias.* Paris: La Découverte 1986, 73.
Ortoli, Sven, & Nicolas Witkowski. *La Baignoire d'Archimède.* Paris: Seuil, 1996.
_____. *Ibid.* 20.
Ouellet, Pierre. *Voir et savoir.* Montreal: Balzac, 1992.
Poissant, Alain. *Vendredi-Friday.* Du Roseau 1988.
Poulin, Jacques. *Volkswagen Blues.* Québec/Amérique 1984.
_____. *Les Grandes Marées.* Ottawa: Leméac, 1978.
Prigogine, Ilya and Isabelle Stengers. *La Nouvelle Alliance.* Paris: Gallimard, "Folio", 1986 [1979].

Roy, Gabrielle. *Alexandre Chenevert.* Montreal: Beauchemin, 1973 [1954].
Studeny, Christophe. *L'Invention de la vitesse.* Paris: Gallimard 1995.
Virilio, Paul. *Esthétique de la disparition.* Paris: Balland, 1980.

Endnotes

1. This text has been written as part of the works of the study group "Machines, textes et savoirs" (MTS), funded by the CRSH (Conseil de recherche en sciences humaines, Ottawa) and the FCAR (Fond pour les chercheurs et l'avancement de la recherche, Quebec).

2. On this criticism of the myth of science as an absolute paragon of truth, there are numerous works. See, for example, Paul Feyerabend's *Dialogues sur la connaissance*; Bruno Latour's *La Science en action*; Jean-Marc Lévy-Leblond's *L'Esprit de sel*; Pierre Ouellet's *Voir et savoir*; Sven Ortoli & Nicolas Witkowski's *La Baignoire d'Archimède*; Ilya Prigogine & Isabelle Stengers' *La Nouvelle Alliance.*

3. Ortoli, Witkowski 20. All the quotations from works in French were translated into English by Éric de Larochellière.

4. On this issue, readers are referred to my book entitled *L'Ambiguïté américaine*, Montreal, XYZ, 1995. A number of elements of this article (concerning Gabrielle Roy, Réjean Ducharme and Monique LaRue) are partly drawn from it.

5. Studeny 216.

6. Marx 27.

7. In the contemporary novel, the car allows above all a drift which will be both geographical and existential. See for example the following novels: Monique LaRue's *Les Faux Fuyants;* Jacques Poulin's *Volkswagen Blues;* Alain Poissant's *Vendredi-Friday;* or Pierre Gobeil's *Dessins et cartes du territoire.*

8. Generally this mode of thought is opposed to a "mechanical" mode of thought: "Categories of both modes of thought are opposed in an unrelenting head-to-head confrontation: flow answers strength; flexibility, rigidity; horizontality, verticality; continuous renewal, stabilization; circular causality, linear causality," (Mattelart, Mattelart 73). This "fluid mode of thought" is associated with the postindustrial and postmodern society in which the contemporary communication technologies have developed. Read, for example, Philippe Breton & Serge Proulx, *L'Idéologie de la communication.*

9. Mattelart, Mattelart 85.

10. Debray 1991, 395.

11. Marcotte 89.

12. Debray 1992, 324.

13. According to Debray, the term "mediasphere" refers to "an environment of transmission and transport of messages and men, with the methods of intellectual development and diffusion which correspond to it" (Debray 1991, 229).

14. *Ibid.* 214.

15. *Ibid.* 214-215.

16. *Ibid.* 239.

17. *Between Two Ages*, cited by Armand Mattelart, in *La Communication-monde*, 159.

18. Virilio 74.

19. *Ibid.* 71.

20. Prigogine, Stengers 1986 [1979].

The Quebec Author in Question(s) on the Québécois Stage

Guy Teissier
Université Rabelais, Tours, France

For centuries, the theatre has shown actors going about their daily business, especially their professional activities. For the Elizabethan theatre, of course, and particularly for Shakespeare, this was an important source of inspiration. But Golden Age Spain also exploited this theme, attempting to show the great theatre of the world, and Baroque writers were seduced by the theatre of illusion. Later, in our own century, Pirandellian "improvisations" or the theatre of Genêt cast theatre within theatre as the acting of actors, the play of players. The challenge in all these instances has been to convey to the audience what makes the theatre what it is: representation by the most obvious means available, the actors. But in so doing, this approach to theatre left out those processes that are anterior to performance, in particular, the process of composition, itself related to the act of writing. In the theatre, the author seems to disappear behind his or her characters, which are represented by actors. Drama has long left to the novel the task of reflecting on writing, and the novel has taken this job of "mise en abyme" seriously, asking the writer in the process of writing all manner of questions about who the author is and what constitutes writing.

During our century, however, the defining features of genres have faded considerably. Novel and theatre, only a century ago conceived of as heterogeneous, have moved closer together as a result of writers practicing (simultaneously and successively) both genres, as in the recent cases of Samuel Beckett, Marguerite Duras and Michel Tremblay. And the self-examination that has become an integral part of writing in the last five decades has allowed theatre to expand and deepen its field of inquiry. This field is no longer limited to visible representation, but, reaching back to the origins of spectacle, is now opening onto a rediscovery of the dramatic author, and onto a careful questioning of the author on the very act of the creation of drama. In *Abel et Bela* (1971) [Abel and Bela],

Robert Pinget engages in a radical technique to accomplish this, entrusting to two characters/actors the interior monologue (dialogue?) of an author in the process of developing the plot and lines of a play.

Québécois playwrights, fascinated by the technique of theatre within the theatre, have paid particular attention to the problems of who and what the author is, especially during the 80s in the judgment of some critics.

> Dans les années quatre-vingt, la prise de parole et le geste d'écrire se sont individualisés. L'écriture est devenue un thème d'écriture, une activité par laquelle un sujet questionne son propre rapport au réel et à la fiction. Ce débat entre la réalité et la fiction, le faux et le vrai, traduit la volonté d'explorer d'autres champs de conscience, plus proches du désir, des pulsions. C'est comme si, par l'exploration du fantasme, on cherchait à nommer ce qui reste du rapport au réel, une fois convaincu de l'impossibilité d'agir concrètement ou physiquement sur le réel.[1]
>
> [In the 80s, the acts of speaking and writing became matters for self-reflection. Writing became a theme of writing, an activity through which a subject examined his or her own relationship to what is real and what is fiction. This debate between reality and fiction, the false and the true, translates the will to explore fields of consciousness closer to that of desire and of the impulses. It is as if, through the exploration of fantasy, writers were seeking to name what remained of the relationship to the real, once writers were convinced of the impossibility of acting concretely or physically on the real.]

Three plays, which still figure in current Quebec theatre, illustrate, though in radically different manners, this examination of the author during the 80s: *Provincetown Playhouse*, by Normand Chaurette (1981); *Le Vrai Monde?* [*The Real World*?], by Michel Tremblay (1987), and *J'écrirai bientôt une pièce sur les nègres* [*Soon I'll Write a Play about Ghostwriters*], by Jean-François Caron (1989).[2] These theatrical examinations clearly echo the questions Québécois playwrights asked themselves in a decade marked by the disillusionment of the first referendum on independence, and the thinking that resulted from that experience.[3] Slowly, following a period of reflection on the individual and his or her increasing awareness, through art and the act of writing, through questions on the search for beauty, on the relationship of an experimental theatre to the public, or on the personal and psychological motives for dramatic writing, with its excesses, its deformations and borrowings (admitted or not) from immediate reality, points of view resurfaced that were at once more political, more committed, and more militant. As a result, the author-writer developed a substantial corpus of questions to be put to the fictional author (who, in a way, represented the former), that redound upon the spectator. From Chaurette to Tremblay to Caron, the author, by calling the author into question, into many questions, in fact, draws the spectator into reflecting on the nature of theatre writing, not only in Quebec, but everywhere.

PART I: A Psychic and Esthetic Interrogation: Normand Chaurette's *Provincetown Playhouse*, 1981

Its evocative title recalling the well-known American group of artists and experimentalists that began performing in the Massachusetts seaside Wharf Theatre in 1914 and acquainted the public with Eugene O'Neill, *Provincetown Playhouse* "is a play about theatre, beauty, guilt, memory haunted by a crime, real or dreamed, imagined or acted out in the theatre" according to the summary of its author Normand Chaurette.[4] It is "a nest of plays constructed on the principle of theatre within theatre, that has at the same time the suspense of a detective plot and the theme of investigation. There is a constant correlation between the search for truth and the play's scrambling of information, its fictionalizing, its theatralization."[5]

Despite its deep complexity, this play appears, at least upon first reading, to use — traditionally, could it be said? — the world of the theatre. After all, several scenes are devoted to the performance of a show, in a space meant to serve social purposes, produced and performed by actors for an audience. Be that as it may, beyond this reproduction of "representation", the play makes subtle use of multiple dramatic and textual strategies to turn our attention to the act of writing itself.

The protagonist among the four characters of this play, their number actually reduced by alternating appearances, is without question Charles-Charles, simultaneously author of the text *L'Immolation de la Beauté* [The Sacrifice of Beauty], director of this same play, "actually" performed in 1919, and one of its actors. But suffering from the effects of "madness", he splits into two characters, one living in 1919, one living 19 years later in 1938. In fact, this temporal partition recedes in importance, and we witness instead a dialogue between two parts of a single individual, one recalling the past of the 1919 performance, the other revealing what happened between that performance and the individual's internment in an insane asylum in Chicago.

Taking on multiple functions in the show, Charles-Charles in both his appearances (1919 and 1938) is seen first as the director of the acting company responsible for the performance of July 19, 1919, but then, and more importantly, as director and manager of a performance that, because of frequent interruptions, takes on the appearance of a rehearsal (with all the repetitions a rehearsal involves, to the point that Tableau 9 of the play becomes a caricature). Yet Charles-Charles also claims the status of author in Tableau 13 (Chaurette 87-90). Indeed, if Chaurette's play appears to deal with a fatal incident, the assassination of a Black child during the performance of an obscure and vaguely ritualistic play, Chaurette emphasizes that "la pièce se passe dans la tête de l'auteur, Charles-Charles [the play takes place in the head of the author, Charles-Charles].

During the play, for which Chaurette relies upon the performance, remembered and even restituted in fragments, of *L'Immolation de la beauté*, the theatre is called into question at several points, not only by the audience, but also by the judges charged with hearing the trial for the child's murder.[6] These latter express conventional ideas on art and the theatre, far removed from the "maniacal" convictions of Charles-Charles.

> Ce qu'on nous reprochait le plus, c'était l'exultation. Défaut notoire, qui nous distinguait, Alvan, Winslow et moi, de ces autres fumistes dont le théâtre n'avait d'autres recours qu'à de tristes et médiocres pensées. Nos vues étaient plus audacieuses; nous disions que le théâtre était nos vies. Hélas, trop pris dans le dédale de l'Art, Alvan et Winslow furent les derniers à se rendre compte que nous dérangions. Quant à moi, je savais, dès le début, que même au théâtre un enfant ne pouvait être éventré sans susciter quelque rumeur (Chaurette 79).
>
> [We were most severely reproached for our exultation. A noteworthy fault, distinguishing us, Alvan, Winslow and me as it did from those other phonies who used only sad and mediocre ideas for their theatre. Our vision was more daring. We claimed that the theatre was our life. Ah, but too deep into the maze of Art, Alvan and Winslow were the last to realize that we were upsetting people. As for me, I knew from the start that, even in the theatre, a child can't be slaughtered without arousing suspicion.]

Presenting his text as avant-garde and exploratory theatre (and the lines in *L'Immolation de la beauté* have undertones of esoteric symbolism, which Chaurette caricatures), Charles-Charles defends his "hermetic" (Chaurette 45) play, and the ambitions of non-commercial theatre. For in the face of the dramatic sacrifice, which is in fact carried out and becomes an onstage murder, the audience, like the judges, no longer sees this play as anything other than the "work of a madman" (Chaurette 36). Charles-Charles, on the other hand, affirms that it is "le théâtre de la vérité" (Chaurette 35, 36) [theatre of the truth], drawing comparisons with a boxing match (Chaurette 44). But he makes an even greater appeal to Greek tradition, on which European and Occidental theatre is founded. Atreus sacrificed the children of Thyestes medea her own sons; and during the Trojan war, the Greeks slaughtered Iphigenia, Polyxena, and Hector's son. At one point in the play, the author says, "Immolation. Le théâtre doit renouer avec la tradition grecque. L'enfant s'appelait Astyanax. Relisez vos classiques" (Chaurette 46). [Sacrifice. Theatre needs to renew its ties to Greek tradition. The child's name was Astyanax. Read your classics].

By putting these exaggerated statements in the mouth of his character (is he truly mad, we might well ask ourselves?),[7] is Chaurette not availing himself of the opportunity to ask theatre, and the author of theatrical productions, essential questions on the role of the spectator-voyeur, as well as that of the sado-masochistic author, both associated in a project comprising nothing but a fragile balance between the revelation of fantasies and the cruelest of impulses, on the one hand, and their sublimation through writing and art, on the other hand? And for what kind of theatre, what form? That is the question that bedevils Charles-Charles the author (but could it also perplex Chaurette?).

By situating his play in the United States during the 20s and 30s, Chaurette has placed his central character far from Quebec's problems of the moment, far from himself, above all. He gave Charles-Charles no explicit feature of his own biography, as far as can be seen. But the figure of the author has haunted Chaurette from the outset of his career of theatre writing. His first play, *Rêve d'une nuit d'hôpital*[8] [Dream of a Night in a Hospital], his début in 1976, presented the Québécois poet Émile Nelligan and excerpts from his work, though the process of writing is not dealt with onstage. But the insanity that formed the central concern of this play reappears, linked this time to writing for the theatre, in Chaurette's third play, *Provincetown Playhouse.*[9]

If a model for Charles-Charles must be sought, it would probably be found in the theatre of Antonin Artaud. Through his search for a theatre of "cruelty", Artaud's book, *Le Théâtre et son Double* [*The Theatre and its Double*], published coincidentally in 1938, influenced directors the world over during the 70s. It is not without interest that Artaud, heavily drugged and ill, was hospitalized in Rodez in 1939.

However, in its plot development, the play seems to hide the moment of writing, though it continually brings up theatrical techniques, both scriptural and scenographic. In any case, for the individual who comes upon the play in the edition published by Leméac in 1981, the variants given at the end of the book are of particular interest. This practice, totally unexpected in a theatre text today, is normally reserved for scholarly and critical editions. In his "Note de l'Auteur" [Author's Note], Chaurette justified the extension of his text beyond the limits of the portion meant for the stage:

> J'ai fait deux versions de *Provincetown Playhouse* (...) La première version fait vaguement allusion à certains moments de ce qui aurait pu être le *Théâtre de l'Immolation de la beauté*, mais l'écriture se trouve à confondre les deux pièces; et je conçois volontiers qu'une telle superposition exige beaucoup quant aux possibilités de la représentation.
>
> Néanmoins, la lecture de *Provincetown Playhouse* m'apparaîtrait incomplète en faisant abstraction de sa version originelle, dont voici, sous forme de variantes, les tableaux qui ont été modifiés. Il s'agit des tableaux 6 à 13.
>
> [I wrote two versions of *Provincetown Playhouse* (...) The first one makes vague allusions to certain moments in what might have been the *Theatre of the Sacrifice of Beauty*, but as it turns out, writing mixes the two plays; and I can see that such a superposition demands quite a bit as far as performance possibilities are concerned.
>
> Nonetheless, I think that a reading of *Provincetown Playhouse* would seem incomplete without the modified tableaux of the original version, that is six through thirteen, here presented as variants.]

In fact, Chaurette gives only tableaux 6 and 11 that emphasize the act of writing. Tableau 11 lists a few considerations on the style of the play *L'Immolation de la Beauté*, not yet performed, but only cited. The tone might be considered humorous, even self-deprecatory, referring as much to Charles-Charles's play as to Chaurette's text:

> Voyez-vous, la pièce comportait certaines répliques qui avaient, si j'ose dire, un pouvoir hypnotique---par exemple, j'avais passé des jours et des jours à étudier et à récrire la scène du partage sacré qui prenait tout son sens caché dans les mots qui sonnaient très curieusement lorsqu'on les mettait les uns à côté des autres... j'avais voulu créer un effet soporifique... la hurleuse s'est endormie...d'un certain point de vue, c'était donc réussi...un peu trop peut-être... d'ailleurs, si on y pense bien, tout a été un peu trop réussi dans la pièce.[10]
>
> [You see, the play contained certain lines that had, if I may say, a hypnotic power...(F)or example, I spent days and days studying and rewriting the scene with the sacred portion, whose hidden meaning came from words that sounded very strange when put side by side. (I) tried to create a soporific effect...the screamer had fallen asleep...so from a certain point of view, it was successful...perhaps too successful... (A)nyway, if you really think about it, everything in the play was a little too successful].

But it is the original Tableau 6 that places the author in the act of writing on-stage. A progressive unfolding of Charles-Charles's insanity comes to a climax, as this character, panicked by the sight of the blank page, attempts to write Tableau 6 of his own play:

> J'ai décidé d'écrire n'importe quoi. N'importe quoi. Quand on est fou, les choses se passent très vite dans une tête. J'ai écrit la première intrigue qui m'est passée par la tête. Puis je l'ai rayée. J'avais l'obsession d'en finir avec ce sixième tableau, il fallait absolument que je règle le cas du sixième tableau c'était obligatoire pour mettre un point final à ma pièce après ça tout serait plus facile une fois celui-là écrit les autres viendraient par la force des choses mais celui-là c'était épouvantable les idées me fuyaient j'avais peur d'être un écrivain raté alors je me suis cogné la tête sur ma feuille blanche et j'ai crié QUE LE DIABLE EMPORTE LE SIXIÈME TABLEAU j'ai écrit "Leur dire que je suis fou" j'ai rayé j'ai écrit encore une fois j'ai rayé j'ai dit c'est là qu'ils vont se rendre compte que l'auteur est malade qu'il va finir ses jours dans une clinique c'est la seule fin plausible à la pièce et ils vont se dire que le sixième tableau

> aurait mieux valu jamais l'écrire...le sixième tableau ...le sixième tableau... ...le sixième tableau... (Effrayé devant la page blanche, il pleure en silence.) [11]
>
> [I decided to write just anything. Anything. When you're crazy, things happen quickly in your head. I wrote the first story that came to my mind. Then I scratched it out. I was obsessed with finishing this sixth tableau, I absolutely had to take care of this sixth tableau it was strictly necessary in order to put a period at the end of my play. After that everything would be easier once that was written the others would come as a matter of course, but that tableau it was horrible ideas escaped me I was afraid of being a failed writer so I banged my head against the blank page and I yelled TO HELL WITH THE SIXTH TABLEAU I wrote "Tell them I am crazy" I crossed it out I wrote again I crossed out I said this is where they are going to see that the author is a sick man that he's going to end up in a hospital that's the only plausible end to the play and they're going to think that the sixth tableau he would have been better off never writing it...the sixth tableau...the sixth tableau......the sixth tableau...(Overcome with fear at the sight of the blank page, he weeps in silence.)]

The coincidence of the number 6 between Charles-Charles's play and Chaurette's seems to point to a convergence of the two authors, the fictional one and the real one, since Chaurette, no more than his character, cannot (or rather will not), in this first draft, write a dramatic episode to answer to what he calls the public's "need for a plot".

> Je voulais tout donner, alors au sixième tableau, il fallait qu'il se passe quelque chose sinon les gens allaient sortir. Pour un auteur c'est la mort. C'est le coup de couteau dans le ventre.
>
> J'ai vécu des angoisses abominables en écrivant ma pièce. Arrivé au sixième tableau, j'ai été assailli des doutes les plus effrayants. Est-ce qu'ils vont s'apercevoir que le théâtre est de moins en moins accessible? [12]
>
> [I wanted to give it my all, so in the sixth tableau, something had to happen or else people would get up and leave. For an author, that's death. It's a knife in your gut.
>
> I had horrible anxieties while I was writing my play. When I got to the sixth tableau, I was overcome by the most terrible doubts. Are they going to see that theatre is less and less accessible?]

To simplify matters for the director and the audience, in the final version (for the stage), Chaurette replaced this crisis of writing with a scene that is constantly interrupted and begun again, to the point that Charles-Charles states with great assurance (should we understand this to be a transposed reminder of the first tableau 6?) : "Cette pièce n'a qu'un début."[13] [This play has only a beginning]. And to be sure, the viewer who sees the beginning of Charles-Charles's play, and hear (repeatedly) the first lines of it, will know nothing of the subsequent tableaux, mentioned only in the narrative of Charles-Charles in Tableau 10.[14]

But the author Normand Chaurette, who reworked his play so that it would be playable and theatrical, who overcame his refusal to put the play (even reduced to a few lines) of his insane author in his own play, who moved the center of his text on writing-creation to the representation-creation of the theatre, did not wish to cast aside the essence of his text, and communicated it to his reader, at least, establishing by this act a two-layered work where the viewer is invited to witness an examination of the spectacle, while the reader is increasingly bound up in the agonies of writing. Unless Chaurette, who inserted excerpts from *Mémoires* [Memoirs] by Charles-Charles between several tableaux, thus posing the problem of integrating them in the staging of these narrative texts, is also suggesting that the material relegated to the variants could be used, integrated into a staging of the play, and be dreaming— who knows?—that the first version (the appendix) could also be staged, just as a way to implicate the viewer further in the fabrication by an author (Normand Chaurette) of this drama by the author (Charles-Charles) confronting writing.

PART II: A Moral and Technical Questioning: Michel Tremblay's *Le Vrai Monde?* [*The Real World*?]

In the specifically Montrealese universe of Tremblay's plays, *Le Vrai Monde?* first performed in 1987, relatively late in Tremblay's career, is no exception. Once again, he uses "very ordinary" scenes of family life somewhere on the Mont Royal Plateau. Yet the primary question in this play is the question of the theatre. In its very form, the play evokes in

Pirandellian fashion the appearance in real life of characters who step out of an author's manuscript to act out their dramas.

The pivotal character is Claude, who is the only character to remain on-stage for the duration of the play. This 23 year-old, an unenthusiastic printer,[16] aspires to be a writer. He has already written a play which he has given to his mother to read. From this manuscript (which may possibly be performed later) emerge stage characters: doubles, barely caricaturized, of the real family, of the "vrai monde" [real world], of the mother Madeleine, the father Alex, and Mariette the sister. The spectator witnesses the actions of two families, the one from real life (series 1) that speaks with Claude and of which he is a member, and the one from the theatre (series 2) that, reconsidered and remodeled by Claude, is unaware of his presence and acts as if he were not there. It is assumed that the audience is witnessing the performance of a text actually composed by Claude, or more likely, an improvisation based on the intentions of his play. We see onstage a Madeleine II, an Alex II, and a Mariette II, but no Claude II.

This "theatrical presentation" (if we may so call an "incarnation" of a text that is far removed from any traditional theatre performance where actors are, by definition, expected to be onstage) permits Madeleine I, the privileged reader, and subsequently other members of the family, who have incidentally not read the manuscript, to formulate their critiques. There are questions about how the young author, according to his family, transformed family reality under the pretext of revealing its profound truth hidden beneath silence and decorum, which put the son-writer on trial, judged by the real life characters of his family.

But beyond the plot and the case against Claude, there is also another, more general trial that the author (and here the author is Michel Tremblay) conducts on how dramatic art functions, and on its own processes of inspiration and creation.

"*Le Vrai Monde?* est en effet une pièce sur le théâtre dans le théâtre, sur le rapport entre la réalité et la création et sur le droit de l'artiste à se servir du réel pour en créer une fiction" [*Le Vrai Monde?* is in fact a play on theatre within theatre, on the relationship of reality to art and on the right of the artist to use what is real to create what is fictional], acknowledges Tremblay.[17] Throughout the play, Claude responds by defending himself when he is reproached for his play, and how it was composed. His mother Madeleine, after all the closest to him and to his feelings, first accuses him of having treated members of the family as if they were fictional characters. In fact, Claude faithfully copied the reality of "his world", down to its minute details, (it is simple enough for Madeleine to recognize "les meubles, les draperies, le tapis usé devant la porte, la télévision Admiral" (Tremblay 23), [the furniture, the drapes, the threadbare carpet at the door, the Admiral television set] as well as the accessories of a dress or a hair style. With the same realist method, without any transposition, he claims to expose the family's problems: the relationship between the mother and the father, between the father and the daughter.[18]

This staging of family relationships, brought to life through Claude's careful observation, causes him to be accused of "curiosité morbide" (Tremblay 86) [morbid curiosity], and even of spying (Tremblay 48, 79). Recognizing at least in part the validity of the reproach: "C'est peut-être vrai que c'est du travail d'espion, en fin de compte, que j'me sus servi de tout c'que j'pensais savoir sur vous autres pour dire des choses qui sont pas agréables à entendre" (Tremblay 51), [Maybe it is true, after all, that it's espionage, that I used everything I thought I knew about you people to say stuff that is not pleasant to hear], Claude attempts to justify himself, using the traditional means of playwrights: "Tous les écrivains font ça, maman, prendre des choses autour d'eux pis les restituer de la façon qu'y les voient, eux..." [All writers do that, Mom, they take what's around them and put it back together in the way they themselves see it...] (Tremblay 50).

At the same time, Madeleine accuses her son of having made them into caricatures, "made them ugly" by transforming particular elements of their existence, for example, changing the music she listens to.[19] Claude's fusion of resemblances and deformations troubles his inexperienced mother-reader, and Claude tries again, clumsily, to be sure, to explain the difference between reality and theatralization: "C't'un personnage de théâtre... Y'est pas dit nulle part que c'est exactement toi..." (Tremblay 23). [It's someone up there on the stage... It's not said anywhere that it's exactly you...] In this rather simple exchange on realism and the imaginary world, basic ideas on the right of the author stand out: can the author use the world around him or her to make an identical twin copy, applying creative techniques to make it all theatrical?

Bit by bit, the questions hone in on the motives for this dramatization, which has truly transposed family life into "dramas". For where the mother, father, and sister claim to lead a very ordinary existence, Claude's play creates some conflagratory situations, presenting a second household, complete with wife and child, that Alex maintains while he is away on sales trips. The play also shows Madeleine's objection and her revolt, which lead to a break-up of the relationship. In the second part of the play, Claude exposes the incestuous impulses that presumably led Alex to his daughter's bed for a rape that failed, and that push him furthermore into the bar where she works as a go-go dancer.

With varying degrees of conviction, each character contests these interpretations, and accuses Claude of fantasizing, of projecting his own inhibitions onto family reality: "C'est tes problèmes à toi...que t'as réglés dans c'te pièce-là, pas les miens" (Tremblay 44). [It's your own problems you solved in this play, not mine.] On the other hand, Claude claims that he wanted to say certain things once and for all: "j'essaye de trouver un sens à ce qui se passe à l'intérieur des autres" (Tremblay 25). [(I)'m trying to find meaning to what happens inside others]. By replacing the "vrai monde" [real world], the one that is reality, made up of appearances, of false fronts, of what is not said, a world made up of lies, with the "monde vrai" [true world], which is to say, the naked, uncompromisingly exposed world, Claude tried to answer questions he felt had been left hanging, particularly the attitude of his father toward his mother, as well as toward his sister Mariette, and still more particularly, toward him, Claude, who claims he wrote the play, in fact, to "speak" to his father.[20]

It is true, however, that Madeleine is justified in articulating a serious criticism of Claude's play when she reproaches him for not having put himself on-stage:

> T'as parlé de tout le monde, dans' famille, sauf de toi. C'est à dire que les personnages parlent de toi, mais t'es pas là. Jamais. Comment ça se fait, ça? (...) Quand on a fini de lire ça, on le sait pas qui c'que t'es! T'as faite de nous autres des portraits effrayants, t'as arrangé la réalité comme tu voulais, comme ça faisait ton affaire, t'as même gardé nos noms, Claude, mais tu t'es caché, toi (Tremblay 48).
>
> [You talked about everyone in the family except yourself. What I mean is the characters talk about you, but you're not there. Ever. How does that happen? (...) When we finish reading the thing, we don't know who it is you are. You made some awful portraits of the rest of us, you arranged reality like you wanted, like you needed it to be, you even kept our names, Claude, but yourself you hid.]

While the play presents observations Claude patiently collected from his family, his judgments, his biases, his hypotheses and his theories, in fact the whole universe of his subjectivity in confrontation with the universe of his family, he pretends to be absent, letting the three other members of the family make "his" theatre, as if he were not involved at all.

> Le personnage de Claude auteur est absent de sa pièce, et c'est par cette faille dramatique que s'engouffrent toutes les hypothèses. L'auteur n'a pas de regard sur lui-même ni sur sa propre création. (...) Dehors et quand même dedans, Claude fait les frais de son non-engagement personnel.[21]
>
> [The character of Claude author is absent from his play, and this dramatic breach engulfs all hypotheses. The author does not look at himself or at what he has created. On the outside, and even so on the inside, Claude pays the price of his personal non-commitment.]

This objectivity, which is only apparent, is denounced by Madeleine, and even more by Alex and Mariette, who accuse Claude of having distorted the facts, of having interpreted them out of hatred for his father, for psychological motives, first of all, but also for reasons that go beyond the personal case of Claude, and have to do with dramatic writing in general.

A young playwright, an inexperienced beginner, Claude has not mastered the rules of dramatic writing, probably under the pressure of his family, professional and sexual problems. On the one hand, he has fallen into the trap of a realism that cannot detach itself from the real object, and that copies too "faithfully" the family context, as an oedipal response. On the other hand, he has not been able to avoid dramatic exaggeration:

> La pièce de Claude ne fait pas le détail. En brisant le silence, elle noircit des faits qui n'étaient peut-être que grisâtres. Comme si la parole, une fois amorcée, ne pouvait plus s'arrêter et entraînait Claude vers l'excès.[22]
>
> [Claude's play does not deal with the small things. In breaking the silence, it darkens a picture that was perhaps only gray. As if speech, once initiated, could not be stopped, and pulled Claude into excess.]

For dramatization carries its own dangers. Claude recognizes that he has composed "une...version de la réalité" (Tremblay 49) [one... version of reality]. But writing a play, as Madeleine suggests, is choosing a "more interesting" version of reality, that is, a more dramatic, even melodramatic, version, to the point of fabricating it completely, if reality is not theatrical enough. And it is also proposing utopian solutions, no doubt attractive, but that go nowhere in the end:

> Ta femme, là, dans la pièce, là, qui porte mon nom pis qui-est habillée comme moi, que c'est qu'a' va faire le lendemain matin? Hein? Après avoir joué l'héroïne? On sait ben, ça t'intéresse pas, toi! Quand a'l'ouvre la porte pis qu'a' sort d'la scène, a'l'arrête d'exister pour toi pis tu t'en sacres, d'abord que t'as écrit des belles scènes! Mais moi, faut que je vive demain, pis après-demain, pis les autres jours (Tremblay 43-44).
>
> [That woman, in the play there, who has my name and wears clothes like I have, what's she gonna do tomorrow morning? Huh? After she plays the heroine? We know, it doesn't make any difference to you! When she opens the door and leaves the play, she stops existing for you, and you don't give a damn, once you've written your fine scenes! But I gotta live tomorrow, and the day after and all the days after.]

This reinterpretation of reality can lead an author who lacks feelings to transform facts in order to make them fit for the theatre. If in the first part of the play, Alex's affair with Madame Cantin de Sorel seems to exist in reality (Madeleine only questions the reaction of her theatrical double when she finds out about this betrayal), nothing in the second part of the play authenticates Claude's version of Alex's equivocal (according to Claude) feelings for his daughter. Mariette systematically refutes the allegations of her brother, whom she accuses of jealousy.

> La dramatisation des discours devient manifeste dans la fiction où ils explosent autour de la quête de la vérité et à propos de la façon dont les événements passés ont été reçus.[23]
>
> [The dramatization of discourses becomes manifest in fiction where they explode on the matter of the search for truth and to how past events have been understood.]

The text makes numerous allusions to the connections between Michel Tremblay, experienced and revered author who creates *Le Vrai Monde?* and Claude, a clumsy novice at work on his first play.

Il est difficile de ne pas chercher le Claude absent du côté de Tremblay lui-même. Trop de curieuses coïncidences y invitent. Comment ne pas penser donc au jeune Tremblay des *Belles-Soeurs*, qui, en 1965, se levait et osait parler dans sa langue en plaçant sur la scène du monde des personnages qui n'y avaient pas encore trouvé place?

Nous sommes alors en face de l'auto-analyse d'un auteur.

L'ancien typographe pose un regard lucide et sans doute amusé sur le microcosme familial secoué par la naïveté cruelle de celui qui s'attache à faire surgir sa vérité, au moyen d'effets de théâtre parfois un peu appuyés.

Vingt ans plus tard, devenu spectateur de sa propre audace, Tremblay ne médite-t-il pas sur une exclusion qui l'a consacré écrivain et qui le renvoie à sa difficulté à parler de lui-même, sinon à travers le croisement de figures multiples qui finissent par ressembler à une identité?[24]

[It is difficult not to seek the missing Claude in Tremblay himself. Too many strange coincidences invite us to do so. How can we not think of the young Tremblay of the *Belles-Soeurs* (*The Sisters-in-Law*), who stood up and dared to speak in his language in 1965, putting on the world stage characters who had not yet found their place there?

We seem, then, to be dealing with the author's self-analysis.

The former typographer is looking with lucidity and probably some amusement upon the family microcosm shaken by the cruel naïveté of someone involved in making his own truth come out by means of theatrical effects that are at times somewhat labored.

Twenty years later, having become a spectator of his own audacity, is Tremblay not meditating on an exclusion that made him a writer officially, and that leads him back to his difficulty in speaking about himself unless it can be through the interaction of multiple characters that end up looking like an identity?]

This play asks the author questions on the techniques of dramatic writing, but also and especially on its moral import. Tremblay judges Claude first of all. That is to say, in a way, he judges what he was (or could have been) when he started out twenty years before. But he is also trying to answer certain questions that gnaw incessantly at his writer's consciousness.

> En dévoilant ses choix, en les dénonçant, en exhibant bien comment ils participent de l'invention mais aussi des modestes déguisements de l'imaginaire dès lors qu'il a été décidé que nous sommes au théâtre, Tremblay sourit des roueries naïves de Claude, auteur débutant qui endimanche ses propos quand il le croit nécessaire, mais aussi des siennes propres.[25]
>
> [In revealing his choices, denouncing them, showing how they are part of the invention but also part of the modest disguises of the imaginary world once it was clear that we are in the theatre, Tremblay is smiling at the naïve cunning of Claude, the author who dresses up his comments when he thinks it necessary, but also at his own cunning.]

And in a half-bitter, half-sweet admission to his father, we hear the barely disguised avowal of Tremblay, uncontested master of Québécois theatre and author of spicy "family" novels, wondering about the legitimacy of this interpretation-exploitation of his "real world", which made the creation of most of his work possible.

> J'ai fait ce qu'on appelle...un transfert...C'est ça mon rôle...j'pense. De faire dire aux autres c'qu'y sont pas capables de dire pis ce que chus pas capable de dire moi non plus. Mais chus pus sûr d'avoir le droit de devenir écrivain. Maintenant, j'ai peur de devenir aussi manipulateur que toi. J'ai peur de devenir un conteur de jokes, moi aussi (Tremblay 105).
>
> [I did what is called...a transfer...That's my role, I believe. To make others say what they aren't capable of saying, and what I'm not capable of saying myself either. But I'm not certain anymore of having the right to become a writer. Right now, I'm afraid of becoming as much a manipulator as you. I'm afraid I, too, will become a teller of jokes.]

For so long, he was careful not to represent himself in his real dimensions in his work. Now, in his work of intimate confession, freed of his inhibitions and complexes, Michel Tremblay finally appears as a character.

PART III: A Social And Political Inquiry: Jean François Caron's *J'écrirai bientôt une pièce sur les nègres* [*Soon I Will Write a Play About Ghostwriters*] [26]

With its ambiguous and provocative title (*nègres* referring to Blacks, first of all, but also, and particularly in this title, referring to ghostwriters), J. F. Caron's second play, presented by the Théâtre des Quat'Sous in September 1989, clearly recycled some of the methods Michel Tremblay used in *Le Vrai Monde?*, but more systematically and with greater complexity. In so doing, the young author could approach the problems, particularly social and political ones, faced by the (Québécois) author in a more general manner, translating them for the stage on several levels.

The architecture of this play involves three overlapping levels: to the "reality level" and "theatre level", Caron adds the "novel level". We should, in fact, add another level that would take into account a haunting character who intrudes uncontrollably into the protagonist's work, but who, in the end, comes clearly into focus and joins together the other levels. But more of that later.

As with Chaurette and Tremblay, the central character of Caron's play is a writer,[27] Danny Gaucher, dramatic author. So the almost thirty year-old character is defined on the "reality level". But the tripartite structure of this play multiplies this protagonist. An author three times over, he presents the multiple and complementary facets of the author's situation.

At the level of theatre, meaning the play written by Danny Gaucher which is being enacted for the viewer, and intrudes into the reality level, Gaucher is defined as a "twenty-eight year-old novelist" who has written the novel *Danny-les-Vidanges* [Danny the Sewage]. But the novel the author Gaucher reads in the theatre incarnation of the manuscript written by Danny Gaucher the dramatic author, is enacted and incarnated also. It offers the character of Danny, "about thirty, dramatic author who is working as a garbage man". The protagonist himself summarizes this complex and circular structure:

> Danny Gaucher a écrit une pièce dans laquelle le personnage central, Gaucher --- y a pas qu'un chien qui s'appelle Fido --- écrit un roman, *Danny-les-Vidanges*. Dans lequel le personnage central, Danny, vient d'abandonner l'écriture pour se consacrer désormais à son tout nouveau dada: éboueur.[28]

> [Danny Gaucher has written a play in which the central character, Gaucher --- there's more than one dog named Fido in this world, isn't

there? --- is writing a novel, *Danny-les-Vidanges*. In which the central character, Danny, has just given up writing to devote himself to his latest hobby: being a garbage man.]

In this way, the same character is represented three times — played by the same actor — always as an author: playwright in "reality", novelist in the "theatre", and once again playwright in the "novel". In his stage directions, Caron has this to say about the fragmentation of the character:

> Au point de départ, il y a Danny Gaucher. Au point d'arrivée, il y a Danny. Pour aller chercher Danny, Danny Gaucher a dû passer par Gaucher. On peut parler du même personnage dans trois états différents. Les noms au complet représentent la *réalité*, premier niveau. Les noms représentent le *théâtre*, second niveau. Les prénoms représentent le *roman*, troisième niveau.
>
> Paradoxalement, et ce, même si je nomme les niveaux tels que je les nomme, le véritable niveau *réel* est celui que j'appelle *roman*. C'est qu'il contient la vérité que cherche l'auteur dramatique, enfouie sous les couches de mensonges ou les masques qu'il faut soulever pour l'atteindre. Ainsi, pourrait-on sentir les personnages plus *théâtralisés* dans les niveaux *réalité* et *théâtre* et, pourquoi pas, plus vrais que nature dans le niveau *roman*.[29]
>
> [In the beginning, there is Danny Gaucher. In the end, there is Danny. To get Danny, Danny Gaucher had to go through Gaucher. We could say it is the same person in three different states. The full names represent *reality*, first level. The last names represent the *theatre*, second level. The first names represent the *novel*, the third level.
>
> Paradoxically, even if I called the levels what I called them, the true *real* level is the one I call *novel*. That is the level that contains the truth the dramatic author is looking for, buried under layers of lies, or masks you have to remove to get to that truth. That explains why you might sense that the characters are more *theatralized* in the *reality* and *theatre* levels, and --- why not? --- truer than nature in the *novel* level.]

The author is not the only character onstage. Two others appear with him. To begin with, there is his girl friend, successively a student (Edith Francoeur), an actress (Francoeur), and a nurse (Edith). She reads

Danny Granger's manuscript, and gives her opinions on writing, theatre and politics. And more importantly, there is a third man, Henri Poisson, "dramatic author" also on the *reality* level, Poisson, an editor on the *theatre* level, and Uncle Henri, ex-professor on the *novel* level. In all his many personifications, he is opposed by the central character on matters which, by touching on the conflict between generations and problems of power, deal consistently with the thematics of writing, not so much from the point of view of aesthetics, as from a social and political perspective.

When *J'écrirai bientôt une pièce sur les nègres* opens, Danny Gaucher, dramatic author, has given the manuscript of his play to his girl friend, the student Edith Francoeur, to read.[30] Rather like Tremblay's *Le Vrai Monde?*, but in a more linear fashion, the text of the manuscript is visibly acted out in short sequences interrupted by intrusions from the *reality* level.

In the first part of his play, Caron gives great weight to the "commercial" problems confronting the author, particularly those of the publishing world. In Danny Gaucher's play, Gaucher, an unrecognized young novelist has kidnapped Poisson, the publisher who rejected the manuscript of his novel, *Danny-les-Vidanges*, offering a perfect opportunity to put (Québécois?) publishing on trial:

> Gaucher: À toutes les fois que je présente un manuscrit à quelqu'un (vous, par exemple), on dirait que ce quelqu'un-là (vous, par exemple) s'attend à tenir entre les mains --- il est souvent un peu déçu --- l'Oeuvre de la décennie, le Réjean Ducharme s'entend. Seulement moi, si j'étais --- vous, par exemple --- si je dirigeais une maison d'éditions et que je demandais aux jeunes romanciers d'être Réjean Ducharme, aussi génial--- je m'arrangerais pour être, moi aussi, génial ---comme éditeur. Vous, vous dormez depuis dix ans sur une chaise plus confortable que mon lit (Caron 23).

> [Gaucher: Every time I give someone (you, for example) a manuscript, you would think that someone (you, for example) expects --- and that someone is often rather disappointed --- to hold The Work of the Decade in his hands, we're talking Réjean Ducharme. Only if I were --- you, for example ---, if I headed a publishing house and asked young novelists to be Réjean Ducharme, as great --- I would make it my business to be great, too --- as a publisher. As for you, for ten years now, you've been sleeping on a chair that's more comfortable than my bed.]

But about sixty pages further along, Gaucher triumphantly announces that, having made the rounds of the big Montreal publishers (Leméac, VLB), his novel has been accepted by Boréal, giving Poisson, who had agreed *in extremis* and under pressure to publish the book, the opportunity to respond with an homage to authors, and a celebration of writing:

> Poisson: C'est vrai que je me suis endormi sur place. J'ai décidé de me souvenir pourquoi je suis devenu éditeur. J'ai décidé de devenir éditeur, parce que j'aime les écrivains. J'aime les cervelles détraquées qui s'exorcisent en pattes de mouche. S'abandonner comme un écrivain s'abandonne en période d'écriture, c'est comparable à nul autre abandon que celui d'un délinquant en plein délit. Je vous connais, les écrivains. Vous êtes des casseurs de vitres (Caron 113).
>
> [Poisson: It's true that I fell asleep where I was. I decided to recall why I became a publisher. I decided to become a publisher because I like writers. I like unhinged thinkers that exorcise themselves by scribbling. Letting oneself go like writers let themselves go when they write is like no other letting go except that of a delinquent committing a crime. I know you, writers. You people break windows.]

Following this first confrontation, there is a second one that copies and reflects it. On the "reality level", it deals with the relationship of power, this time not between the writer and the publisher, but between the writer-ghostwriter Danny Gaucher and his superior, the consecrated author:

> Henri Poisson: Je ne comprends strictement rien à: 1) le sujet de ta pièce --- c'est pas ce qu'on s'était dit qu'on ferait; 2) le roman dans la pièce --- le théâtre dans le théâtre --- laissons ça à ceux qui font ben ça; 3) les noms des personnages --- on ne donne pas nos noms à nos personnages (Caron 45-46).
>
> [I don't understand a thing about: 1) the subject of your play --- it isn't what we agreed we would do; 2) the novel in the play --- the theatre within theatre --- let's leave that for the people who do that kind of thing well; 3) the characters' names --- we don't give our characters our names.]

In this conflict, the hour of rebellion has rung. Danny Gaucher, who now wants to write on his own, clearly states this to the person who, until now, has used his talent:

> Tu me demandes, c'est exactement comme ça que ça s'est passé, tu me demandes de t'aider. Ça ressemble à un pacte. Tu me commandes une première pièce que tu corriges et réécris au fur et à mesure pour défaire ce qui est trop moi pis ... coller ça à ta peau. Tu signes. J'encaisse la moitié. Ben fiou! C'est fini. Je veux aucune guerre. Je veux rencontrer le public. Je veux vivre (Caron 54).
>
> [You ask me, this is exactly how it happened, you ask me to help you. It's like a pact. You order a play that you correct and rewrite as you go along so you can get rid of what is too much of me, and ... you make it yours. You put your name to it. I get half the take. Well, phooey! No more of that. I don't want any war. I want to meet the public. I want to live.]

Yet in the novel written by Gaucher (the central character of Danny Gaucher's play), the character of Danny, who is also a dramatic author, adopts a totally different attitude, giving up writing to become a garbage collector and a cesspool cleaner (in English neighborhoods!) Not permanently, of course, "jusse un break que je prends parce que j'en avais mal au bloc d'écrire dans le beurre (Caron 85) [just a break I'm taking because I'm sick and tired of going nowhere with my writing]. But his attitude shows a renunciation, a resignation for which Henri (Uncle) reproaches him vehemently.

Indeed, Caron surrounds Danny with quite divergent opinions on the state of Québécois theatre, "cet océan de tranquillité [that ocean of tranquillity], of declining splendor, according to Henri Poisson, in which finding one's place as a young author can seem difficult. Even a young actress can have her difficulties. It is basically through the lines of the central character's companion, be she student or actress, that Caron articulates his critique of Québéois theatre:

> Le théâtre québécois (sauf exception, corrigez-moi si je fais erreur) a une façon de se regarder le nombril que le théâtre étranger (sauf exception, corrigez-moi) n'a pas (Caron 49).

> [The Québécois theatre (with some exceptions, correct me if I'm wrong) has a way of contemplating its navel that foreign theatre (with some exceptions, correct me) doesn't have.]

In the spirit of these statements, the second part of the play highlights the political problems of Quebec (after the first referendum but before the second one), with the grotesque, scatological entrance of Uncle Henri, a stalwart nationalist and independantist on the *novel* level. Our field of vision is now taken up by the thematics of politics. There is a subtle transition, of course, from the problematics of the writer to those of Quebec, which operates by means of considerations on language and the attempts at independence. But here Caron is dealing with a different subject, using a well-honed sense of dramatic dialectic, entrusting Henri with the nationalist arguments, Danny taking on the task of stating a marginal position, and Edith noting the relativity of Quebec's problem in the context of the universe:

> C'est sûr que moi pis Danny, mononc', on est québécois mais on peut pas jusse être des Québécois. Parce que le Québec appartient au Canada. Le Canada est à l'Amérique du Nord à la Terre, la Terre au système solaire, le système solaire à l'univers, pis on s'en va jusqu'à l'infini (Caron 110).
>
> [It's true, Uncle, that Danny and I are Québécois, but you can't just be Québécois. Because Quebec belongs to Canada. Canada belongs to North America, to Earth, Earth belongs to the Solar System, the Solar System to the Universe, and on you go to infinity.]

When he brings his own questions, his own political doubts to the public, Caron seems far removed from the character of the author of his questions on literature. But perhaps this is not so simple. In fact, to the three levels mentioned, Caron added a fourth:

> Un quatrième niveau s'ajoute aux trois ci-haut mentionnés, mais pas dans l'ordre établi jusqu'ici. Un niveau parallèle, que j'appellerai *Dans la Tête de Danny Gaucher*. Il s'agit de l'espace occupé par Bastarache, un espace intérieur, un espace indéfini. Une voix que Danny Gaucher entend sans trop saisir sa provenance ni même ce qu'elle signifie exactement. Bastarache est comme une bête noire qui rue l'intérieur de l'auteur. Qui veut sortir. Et qui ne laisse pas de répit à son créateur.[34]

> [There is a fourth level to add to the three mentioned previously, but not in the order established so far. A parallel level that I will call *In Danny Gaucher's Head.* This is the space occupied by Bastarache, an interior space, an indefinite space. A voice Danny Gaucher hears without quite knowing where it comes from, or what it means exactly. Bastarache is like a pet peeve that attacks the author's inner self. That is trying to find a way out. And that gives its creator no rest.]

Caron also tried to show the author in the most secret act of composition, like the Charles-Charles in the *Provincetown Playhouse* variants. But while Chaurette's character gave voice to writer's panic and the madness that comes from an inability to fill the void with writing, Caron shows his dramatic author inhabited by an anonymous voice, at first called Bâtard [Bastard], speaking from some unknown place while he transcribes in the manner of the Surrealists, using his typewriter to make sentences the source of which is unknown to him. As Danny Gaucher comments:

> Ce personnage-là me trotte dans la tête depuis deux jours. J'écris. Comme une dictée. Je ne sais rien de lui. Sinon qu'i m'a l'air d'être en prison, d'écrire des missives d'amour. Je le laisse venir tranquillement. I vient, je sais pas d'où, mais je sais qu'i vient d'en d'dans (Caron 45).

> [This character has been trotting around in my head for two days. I'm writing. Like a dictation. I don't know a thing about him. Except that he seems to me to be in prison, like he's writing love letters. I'm just letting him come out. He's coming, I don't know from where, but I know he comes from inside.]

But with the appearance of Henry, on the *novel* level, the mysterious character Bâtard emerges and eventually acquires the identity of Bastarache, which Henri defines as "le premier prisonnier politique, le premier felquiste*" (Caron 64) [the first political prisoner, the first *Felquiste]*. In this way, the most deeply interiorized reflection on the alchemy of writing opens onto a purely political problematic, insofar as

* Translator's Note: A *Felquiste* sympathizes with and/or furthers the aims of the Front de libération du Québec. (See Introduction).

Bastarache comes to Henri's aid in dealing with the battle of the independantists. And to underscore his point, Bastarache demands right away that Danny Gaucher write:

> Bastarache (cri du coeur): Oui! Je veux diriger mon navire! J'ai pus de temps à perdre pis toi non plus! Sonne l'urgence, ouvre les vannes pis écris, ostie! Fais pas semblant! (Caron 72).
>
> [Bastarache (cri du coeur): Yes! I want to steer my own boat! I don't have any more time to lose and you don't either! Press the emergency button, open the floodgates and write, for Christ's sake! Don't just pretend!]

We hear the final celebration of writing as a crime, as terrorism, bringing together all the phases of writing, from composition to publication, not only in its creation, but in the more general and political creation of Quebec. It is as if Caron uses the triple character of the author to analyze and denounce a particular situation, that of the writer, and to articulate metaphorically the Québécois *mal de vivre*. The term "nègre," taken at first in its purely literal sense, thus takes on greater meaning, in the end designating all of Quebec and the Québécois. Shortly after it was finished, Louise Vigeant made this very point:

> Il ne me semble pas arbitraire que l'une des dernières pièces créées récemment, *J'écrirai bientôt une pièce sur les nègres* by Jean-François Caron porte à la fois sur la difficulté d'être créateur et sur l'engagement politique de la jeune génération.[36]
>
> [It does not seem arbitrary to me that one of the most recent productions, *J'écrirai bientôt une pièce sur les nègres* by Jean-François Caron, has to do with the difficulty of being an artist, and with the political commitment of the younger generation, all at the same time.]

Thus, during the course of the 80s, the self-reflection in Québécois theatre succeeded in broadening considerably the traditional field of "theatre within the theatre", broaching subjects and asking questions closer to the act of creation itself, to dramatic writing. From Chaurette, to Tremblay, to Caron, we have seen that each author according to his own sensibilities, and depending as well on his circumstances, has given this inquiry of the author on the author a unique treatment, in each case and at every level initiating an intense search for identity. As Lorraine Hébert observed:

> Tous ces textes traitent de la place du poète dans notre société, des difficultés de la création, de ses élans et aspirations, de ses pouvoirs et de ses limites. (...) [L]'omnipresence de la figure de l'artiste nous force à constater que toute la recherche de l'identité y est reprise à partir du point de départ: dans le geste même de dire.
>
> [All these texts deal with the place of the poet in our society, of the difficulties of creating, of its urges and its aspirations, its powers and its limits. (...) The omnipresence of the character of the artist forces us to recognize that the whole search for identity is repeated here, from the beginning: in the very act of speaking.]

And she concludes:

> Tous les questionnements des années quatre-vingt sur le "je" face au théâtre, à l'écriture, aux mots ont permis à l'auteur de se rendre compte que l'écriture est en soi un geste politique quand on en assume le trajet intime.[37]
>
> [All the questioning during the 80s of the "I" in relationship to the theatre, to writing, to words, gave the author the opportunity to realize that writing is in itself a political gesture when one takes on its deep and intimate trajectory.]

Works Cited and Bibliography

Camerlain, Lorraine. "Jean-François Caron: une histoire qui s'écrit." *Jeu*, 1991/4, December.

Caron, Jean-François. *J'écrirai bientôt une pièce sur les nègres*. Montreal: Les Herbes Rouges, 1990. [*Soon I'll Write a Play About Ghostwriters*.] Translated by Maureen La Bonté. Montréal: Cead Centre des Auteurs Dramatiques, Montreal.

Chaurette, Normand. *Fêtes d'automne*.

_____. *Provincetown Playhouse, juillet 1919, j'avais 19 ans*. Montreal: Leméac, 1981. [*Provincetown Playhouse*.] Translated by William Boulet. Toronto: Coach House Press, 1986.

_____. *Rêve d'une nuit d'hôpital*. Montreal: Leméac, 1980.

Gingras, René. *Le Facteur réalité*. Montreal: Leméac, 1985.

Hébert, Lorraine. Talk presented at the Centre des Auteurs Dramatiques, Montreal. Published in *Jeu 58*, 1991, 1, March.

Messier, J.F.. *Le Dernier Délire permis*. Montreal: Les Herbes Rouges, 1990.

Ryngaert, Jean-Pierre. "Le Vrai Monde?" *Le Monde de Michel Tremblay*. Cahiers de Théâtre, Jeu. Editions Lansman, 1993.

Sadowska-Guillon, Irène. "Michel Tremblay: A la rencontre de soi-même." Remarks collected in *Les Anciennes Odeurs*, *L'Avant Scène Théâtre*, No. 841, January 1, 1989.

_____. "Normand Chaurette / Un art scientifique du langage" [Normand Chaurette / A scientific art of language]. *Acteurs 86-87*. Paris: January-February, 1991.

Tremblay, Michel. *Albertine en cinq temps*. Montreal: Leméac, 1984. [*Albertine in Five Times*.] Translated by John Van Busek and Bill Glassco. Vancouver, B.C.: Talonbooks, 1986.

_____. *Les Belles-Soeurs*. Montreal: Leméac, 1972.

_____. *Le Vrai Monde?*. Montreal: Leméac, 1987. [*The Real World?*.] Vancouver, B.C.: Talonbooks, 1988.

Vigeant, Louise. "Du Réalisme à l'expressionisme - la dramaturgie québécoise récente à grands traits." *Jeu 58*, 1991, 1, March.

Additional Reading:

Brisset, Annie. *A Sociocritique of Translation: Theatre and Alterity in Quebec, 1968-1988*. Translated by Rosalind Gill and Roger Gannon from *Sociocritique de la traduction: théâtre et altérité*. Toronto, Buffalo: University of Toronto Press, 1996.

Usmiani, Renate. *The Theatre of Frustration: Super-realism in the Dramatic Work of F.X. Kroetz and Michel Tremblay*. New York: Garland Press, 1990.

Endnotes

1. Lorraine Hébert in a talk presented at the Center for Dramatic Authors, published in *Jeu 58*, 1991, 1, March., 85.

2. One could also mention *Le Dernier Délire permis* [The Last Delerium Allowed], a play by J. F. Messier "vaguely adapted" from Molière's *Don Juan*, staged in January 1990 at La Licorne, the restaurant theatre, and published by Les Herbes Rouges in 1990. The character of Elvire, transformed into a man, is a novelist, a writer more by calling than by profession. The author gives this information about him:

> "Elvire a écrit un roman qui raconte une tranche de l'histoire qu'il a vécue avec Domme. Au moment où commence la pièce, Elvire est en train de terminer son roman et se prépare à se relire. Tout ce qui suivra sera donc la représentation théâtrale de ce qu'Elvire lit dans les pages de son manuscrit. Il existe donc dans la pièce, une *mise en abyme* où l'on retrouve, à un premier niveau, Elvire qui a fini d'écrire son roman et qui se relit, et au deuxième niveau la représentation de l'histoire que raconte son livre, dont il fait lui-même partie. Ce qui se passe sur scène est-il une représentation de son histoire avec Domme telle qu'il l'a écrite dans son roman, ou au contraire, la représentation de ce qui s'est *vraiment* passé? Libre à chacun de l'interpréter selon son gré. Quoi qu'il en soit, certaines indications dans le texte feront référence à ce changement de niveau. Le premier niveau sera désigné par l'expression 'Niveau roman'. La majeure partie de la pièce se déroule au 'Niveau théâtre', le premier 'Niveau roman' servant surtout de ponctuation et d'ellipse entre les différents temps de l'action. C'est à cause de cette proportion que, sauf exception, seul le 'Niveau roman' sera indiqué" (Messier 8-9). Elvire romancier est donc au début de la pièce (13) "assis devant sa machine à l'une des extrémités du plateau. Il est en train de taper l'avant-derniere page de son roman". Mais cela ne donne, guère de développements sur l'activité propre de l'auteur.
>
> [Elvire has written a novel that recounts part of what he went through with Domme. When the play opens, Elvire is finishing up his novel and getting ready to read it over. Everything that follows is therefore the theatrical representation of what Elvire is reading in his manuscript. There is then in the play a *mise en abyme*, where we find, at an initial level, Elvire who has finished writing his novel and is rereading it, and at the second level the representation of the tale he tells in his book, in which

> he is a participant. Is what we see onstage a representation of his experience with Domme as he wrote it in his novel, or is it rather the representation of what *really* happened? One is left free to interpret the situation as he or she wishes. In any case, certain information in the text will make references to this change in levels. The first level will be designated by the expression "novel level". The greater part of the play occurs on the "theatre level", the first "novel level" serving mostly as punctuation and ellipsis between the various time frames of the action. Because of this proportion, only the "novel level" will, for the most part, be indicated" (Messier 8-9). As the play opens, then, Elvire the novelist is seated in front of his typewriter at one end of the stage. He is typing the next-to-last page of his novel" (Messier, 13).

But this description hardly explains the author's real activity.]

René Gingras's play *Le Facteur réalité* [The Reality Factor], staged at the Théâtre d'Aujourd'hui in 1985, and published by Leméac that year, presents Alain, who is studying literature and dreams of becoming a writer. Obsessed by the work and death of Hubert Aquin, the acclaimed Québécois novelist who died in 1977, he imagines a time when poets had a role in society. The character of André functions as a master of ceremonies and comments on the "Pirandellian" intentions of the author.

> "Pour en revenir à moi-même, et à notre caprice d'auteur, c'est lui justement, qui me demande de vous dire de ne pas trop faire attention: c'est une idée comme ça, qui a quelque chose à voir avec une démarche à lui, très personnelle, "philosophico-formelle", autour de la problématique de la vérité et de l'illusion au théâtre, un questionnement qu'il traîne après lui comme un boulet depuis qu'il a lu un certain Pirandello dans une douteuse traduction française" (Gingras 17). [To get back to me and to our author's little caprice, it is precisely he who asked me to tell you not to be too concerned; it's just one of those ideas, something to do with his approach, very personal, "philosophico-formal", to the problematic of truth and illusion in the theatre, an inquiry he has been dragging around behind him like a ball and chain ever since he read someone called Pirandello in a questionable French translation.]

But the author does not appear as a character onstage.

3. In her article *Du Réalisme à l'expressionisme - la dramaturgie québécoise récente à grands traits* (*Jeu* 58, 1991, 1, March) [From Realism to Expressionism

-Main Features of Recent Québécois Theatre], Louise Vigeant notes that the work of the Bélanger-Campeau Commission:

"en donnant la parole à divers intervenants, dont les artistes --- le rapport présenté par le Conseil Québécois du Théâtre, signé par René-Daniel Dubois, a été remarqué comme l'un des plus percutants --- ont fourni l'occasion d'une réflexion collective non seulement sur le plan de l'organisation politique mais aussi sur l'importance d'une définition claire d'enjeux d'ordre culturel. La place de l'artiste dans notre société a été ainsi rappelée à la mémoire de tous, à juste titre (espérons que l'effet perdurera)" (Vigeant 9). [By letting many speakers, including artists, have a say --- the report presented by the Conseil Québécois du Théâtre (Québécois Theatre Council), signed by René-Daniel Dubois, was thought to be one of the most incisive --- presented an opportunity for collective reflection not only on the level of political organization, but also on the importance of a clear definition of what is at stake as far as culture is concerned. The place of the artist in our society was thus recalled to mind, and rightfully so (let us hope that the effect will last.]

4. Cited by Irene Sadowska-Guillon, "Normand Chaurette / Un art scientifique du langage" [Normand Chaurette / A Scientific Art of Language], *Acteurs 86-87.* Paris: January-February 1991, 80.

5. Ibid. 80.

6. The merger of public and judges is often suggested in the play (see Chaurette 51).

7. In the same way, Antonin Artaud's madness, mentioned in a later paragraph, was questioned.

8. Quebec: Leméac 1980.

9. *Fêtes d'automne* [Autumn Celebrations], Chaurette's second play composed between 1976 and 1982, and presented in 1982 at the Théâtre du Nouveau Monde, similarly mixes together madness and poetic writing.

10. Chaurette. 1981, 121-122.

11. Ibid. 119 - 120.

12. Ibid. 118 - 119. This scene is summarized in a few lines in the final version, 7, p. 59: "Vous savez, j'ai vécu des angoisses abominables en écrivant ma pièce. Par moments, j'ai été assailli des doutes les plus effrayants: est-ce qu'ils vont

s'apercevoir que le théâtre est devenu de moins en moins accessible ...?" [You know, I have gone through abominable anguish writing my play. At times, I was overcome by the most awful doubts: are they going to see that theatre has become less and less accessible ...?]. Lorraine Hébert echoes this concern on the part of Charles-Charles/Chaurette, when she notes that the research of the "new" theatre carries a real "danger de marginalisation" [danger of marginalization]. "Ce type de démarche, d'exigence, n'est jamais populaire. Il faut du temps avant que le sens puisse travailler les masses. Dans la mesure où l'auteur est un détonateur, il ne peut éviter le poids de la marginalité." *Jeu 58*, 1991, 1, March, 85. [This kind of approach, of demand, is never popular. Time has to pass before the meaning can affect the masses. To the extent that the author is a detonator, he cannot avoid the burden of marginality.]

13. Ibid. 57.

14. "Puis au dixième tableau, il est arrivé un autre retardataire. Puis un autre encore . . . à chaque fois, il fallait recommencer la pièce depuis le début. [...] La pièce a continué. On a recréé un climat, de peine et de misère ... Et puis il y a eu la fin ..." (Chaurette 71) [Then in the tenth tableau, another latecomer arrived. Then still another ... each time, the play had to start from the beginning again. [...] The play went on. We recreated a climate of pain and misery ... And then came the end ...]

15. Madeleine, the mother, is Albertine's sister. Present in *Albertine en cinq temps [Albertine in Five Times]*, Tremblay's play published by Leméac in 1984, she is referring here to the homecoming of her husband Alex, a traveling salesman, and to "les p'tits" [the little ones] (Tremblay 1984, 79).

16. "un des métiers les plus plats au monde" [one of the dullest occupations in the world] (Tremblay 1987, 19).

17. Sadowska-Guillon 25-27.

18. "Puisque les vrais et les faux personnages se ressemblent' une partie de leurs discours n'expriment que de légers décalages, signes des inventions légères d'un auteur qui joue avec la réalité" [Since the true and the false characters look alike, part of their discourse expresses only slight differences, signs of the facile inventiveness of an author who is playing with reality] Jean-Pierre Ryngaert, *"Le Vrai Monde?"* in *Le Monde de Michel Tremblay*, Cahiers de Théâtre, Jeu/Editions Lansman, 1993, 199.

19. "La musique que t'as mis là-dedans, j'la connais pas! Pis j'veux pas la connaître! La musique que j'écoute moi, c'est de la musique simple, facile à retenir pis que

j'peux chanter pendant que je l'écoute" (Tremblay 1987, 24). [The music you put in there, I don't know it! And I don't want to know it! The music I listen to, it's simple, easy to remember and I can sing it while I'm listening to it.]

20. "Les premières fois que j'ai pris un crayon pis un papier, j'avais peut-être onze ou douze ans c'était pour te parler/ C'était mon exutoire/ J'ai découvert ... l'exaltation de l'écriture à travers des déclarations d'amour que je faisais à mon père qui voulait rien savoir de moi!" (Tremblay 1987, 100). [The first few times I picked up pencil and paper, I was maybe eleven or twelve, it was to talk to you/ It was my outlet/ I discovered ... the exaltation of writing through the declarations of love I made to my father who didn't want to know anything about me!]

21. Ryngaert 204.

22. Ibid. 202.

23. Ibid. 201.

24. Ibid. 205.

25. Ibid. 198-199.

26. "Personne qui ébauche ou écrit entièrement les ouvrages signés par un écrivain célèbre." [Someone who writes a rough draft or writes entirely works signed by a famous author.] *Dictionnaire Petit Robert*, 1968. While the term does, indeed denote Blacks, its literary sense is made explicit in the course of the play:

> Edith Francoeur - Un jour, une phrase de vous dans une entrevue télévisée. "*J'écrirai bientôt sur les nègres.*" Les quoi? Vous vouliez parler des Noirs? Vous auriez dit "Noirs". J'ai cherché pourquoi vous aviez dit "nègres" [...] Pour quelle raison majeure Danny Gaucher me traînait-il (de force) aux premières de Henri Poisson? Réponse: il me traînait à ses propres premières. Et là, je l'ai reconnu. Sa griffe. Dans vos pièces. Je sais pas quelle était votre méthode, mais je sais que Danny Gaucher était votre nègre" (Caron 50). ["Edith Francoeur - One day, something you said in a television interview. "*I'll write on Negroes soon.*" On what? Were you trying to talk about Blacks? You would have said "Blacks". I tried to figure out why you said "Negroes" [...] What was the chief reason Danny Gaucher dragged me (forcibly) to Henri Poisson's premieres? Answer: he was dragging me to his own premieres. And there I recognized him. His signature style. In your plays. I don't

know what your method was, but I know that Danny Gaucher was your ghostwriter.]

27. On the subject of this obsessive presence of the author, Caron ironically seems to be making a criticism when he has the companion of his hero, Edith Francoeur, say: "L'omniprésence de l'auteur. Je tique. Je veux dire Claudel ne parlait jamais de lui. Toi, tu ne parles que de toi, et ça m'inquiète." (Caron 72). [The omnipresence of the author. I'm wincing. I mean Claudel never talked about him. You, you only talk about yourself, and that worries me].

28. Caron 36.

29. Ibid. 8-9.

30. "Edith Francoeur est étendue sur le lit. Elle lit le manuscrit de Danny Gaucher, c'est à dire l'action qui a lieu plus bas, sur le plancher." (Caron 14). [Edith Francoeur is lying on the bed. She is reading Danny Gaucher's manuscript, that is, the action that is taking place down below, on the stage.]

31. Edith Francoeur says so, as well: "Vous allez devoir écrire vous-même votre prochaine pièce, seul ... ou chercher ailleurs un nouveau jeune auteur." (Caron 48). [You are going to have to write your next play by yourself, alone ... or look for a new young author somewhere.]

32. "'Où en sommes-nous?' demande Caron à ceux de sa génération et aux autres Québécois. Questionnements et points de vue s'entremêlent dans cette pièce en jeu de blocs, sans toutefois que soit proposée une réponse univoque." Lorraine Camerlain, *Jean-François Caron: une histoire qui s'écrit* in *Jeu*, 1991 / 4, December, 13. [Where are we at this point? Caron is asking the members of his generation, and other Québécois. Questionings and points of view intermingle in this building block play, without a univocal response being offered.]

33. "Où suis-je, moi, dans toutes ces contradictions? Au coeur même. Je voulais, pour la première fois de ma vie, que tous mes personnages aient raison. C'était inoculer toutes mes contradictions privées au public. N'était-ce pas là le propos même de ma pièce? N'est-ce pas là ce qu'on fait quand on écrit une pièce de théâtre? Et n'est-ce pas ce qu'on fait quand on va au théâtre? Sortir son privé en public, histoire de ne pas garder ça pour soi plus longtemps? Questions." (Caron 130-131). [Where am I, me, in all these contradictions? In the very heart of them. For the first time in my life, I wanted all my characters to be right. It was like infecting the public with all my private contradictions. Isn't that the very subject of my play? Isn't that what one does when one writes a stage play? And isn't that

what one does when one goes to the theatre? Take his or her private life out in public, so you don't keep all that for yourself any longer? Questions.]

34. Caron 9.

35. Francoeur the actress is the one who develops this theme in a response: "La page blanche, moi, je virerais folle. Ça serait le livre blanc à longueur d'année. Moi, je panique à écrire une lettre. Puis je vois Gaucher faire depuis assez longtemps pour ... Moi, écrire?" (Caron 76) [The blank page, me, I'd go crazy. It would be a blank book all year long. I panic writing a letter. And I've been watching Gaucher work long enough to ... Me, write?]

36. Vigeant 9.

37. Hébert 85.

Québécois Writers of the 1990s: Voices from Elsewhere --- about Elsewhere

Ramon Hathorn
University of Guelph, Ontario

During the nineteenth century, the cities of Quebec and Montreal were ports of call for a steady stream of immigrants, many of whom, mostly of British descent, moved on to Ontario and points west, as well as the United States. After the Conquest of 1760, English officers and troops settled in the St. Lawrence valley, as did a number of Scots; during the early 1800s, Irish peasants fleeing the famine, as well as others from the British Isles, changed the cultural landscape of Montreal so much so that Anglophones of British descent were in the majority from 1831 to 1867, at which point French Canadians flocking to the city from rural communities became once again the dominant group. Even though 98 percent of Montreal's population was of French or British descent during the nineteenth century, ethnic diversification began, though slowly, at the turn of the century with the arrival of Jewish immigration from eastern Europe. In the twentieth century Europeans from Germany, Italy and other countries were followed by numerous groups: for example, Greeks, Portuguese, Ukrainians, Asians such as the Vietnamese, and in the 1970s, Haitians fleeing the Duvalier dictatorship. By 1981 French Canadians formed 66 per cent of the greater Montreal population; those of British descent 11 per cent and other ethnic groups 20 per cent (cf. Linteau, 1988).

Given the large numbers of Anglophones in nineteenth century Montreal, it is not surprising that English-speaking characters appear in the earliest novels written in Quebec. In *Les Fiancés de 1812* (1844) [The Engaged Couple of 1812], Joseph Doutre creates a most positive portrait of Brandsome, an American soldier of Irish descent who is a Republican, anti-British and anti-clerical — qualities that justify his marriage to a French Canadian despite the War of 1812 and that attracted bitter criticism from Francophones opposed to such a match. Both English and Scottish officers play important roles in Philippe-Aubert de Gaspé's novel, *Les Anciens Canadiens* (1863) [*The Canadians of Old*], which recreates scenes from the conquest of Quebec in 1760 and which, like the many historical novels that followed in subsequent decades, depicts the Anglo-Saxon officer as a domineering conqueror. The Roman Catholic Scot, Archibald de Locheill, however, is presented as the victim of racial and religious hatred that has followed him from the glens of Scotland to the Plains of Abraham in the person of Montgomery, a Protestant officer and enemy of his father. In 1922, the eminent nationalist historian, Abbé Groulx, under the pen name of Alonié de Lestres, produced a first novel with racist overtones, *L'Appel de la race* [The Call of Race], which overnight became a best-seller and provoked bitter discussion within the Francophone community. Borrowing partially from two historians, F.-X. Garneau and Augustin Thierry, he describes the House of Commons as "an arena where two races and two civilizations confront and oppose each other" and the bonds of intermarriage as being strained by "two warring souls or spirits", each seeking constantly to dominate. Groulx's use of stereotypes based on the essential incompatibility of "racial" differences is also borrowed in part from Maurice Barrès' *Colette Baudoche (1908)*, whose Alsatian heroine refuses to marry one of the German occupiers of her homeland. *L'Appel de la race* [The Iron Wedge], a French Canadian re-write of the Barrès work, over the next two decades inspired a dozen or so novels in French Canada whose plots focused on the very relevant issue of intermarriage between Anglophone and Francophone. By his denunciation of the Anglo-Saxon female, Groulx prefigures writers of the Quiet Revolution such as Jacques Godbout and Hubert Aquin whose revolutionary protagonists will threaten with violence, death, rape and murder their Anglophone mistresses.

Other than passing references to drunken or thieving Irish, the occasional Black or Métis, immigrants from other cultures have found little place in the fictional landscapes of Quebec since 1844. Yves Thériault is one of the first French Canadian novelists to portray in a sympathetic and serious way Quebec minorities such as the young Orthodox Jewish boy in *Aaron* (1954), the Inuit in *Agaguk* (1958) and aboriginals in *Ashini* (1960). Nor could one forget the Arctic backdrop of *La Rivière sans repos* [*Wind Flower*] (1970) where Gabrielle Roy depicts the Inuit in painful transition, nor her sensitive essays about prairie immigrant communities such as the Mennonites and Doukhobors in

Fragiles Lumières de la terre (1978), available in Alan Brown's excellent translation as *Fragile Lights of Earth* (1982). Only in the 1970s and particularly in the 1980s, do immigrant writers begin to write in French and be published in Montreal, bringing new voices and new perceptions, not only of their respective communities, but also of the new society in which they find themselves. In the 1990s, several novelists, both established and beginners, have received exceptional critical praise and acceptance in the Quebec community. All come from diverse cultural backgrounds; all write in French, as their first language or the one adopted by choice; they all turn their back on the introspective writing traditions of their new land and in so doing, move Quebec literature another step beyond the national (and even nationalistic). Their writings suggest that the Quebec novel may be entering yet another new phase, after so many innovative others in recent years, that could be well described, one might argue, as the refreshing era of post-nationalism.

In the 1980s, one of the new voices heard on the Montreal stage was that of the Italo-Québécois, which not only expressed itself with passion, anger and frustration as vigorous as that expressed by Michel Tremblay's hapless Léopold in *A toi pour toujours, ta Marie-Lou* [*Forever Yours, Marie-Lou*], but confronted head-on the political credos of French unilingualism and assimilation into the culture of the majority. In *Gens du silence* (1982) [People of Silence], Marco Micone examines the exploitation of first-generation immigrants to Montreal, with heavily didactic but nonetheless telling dramatic effect. Nancy, the 26 year old teacher of Italian descent who learned her third language, French, at McGill argues with her friend about the importance of learning French and writing in French. Only in this way will the children of Italian immigrants she teaches find role models that will help them adapt to their new and unwelcoming milieu and perhaps escape a life of slavery in the factories where their parent eke out a meagre living:

> Gino, I teach teenagers who all have Italian names and who have one culture, that of silence. Silence about the peasant origin of their parents. Silence about the manipulation they're victims of. Silence about the country they live in . . . We can't do anything for the parents. We have to find the ways the ghetto-keepers haven't used yet. We must replace the culture of silence by immigrant culture, so that the peasant in us stands up, so that the immigrant in us remembers, and so that the Québécois in us can start to live (65).

Gino, accusing his compatriot of being naïve, argues to the contrary, that a minority beginning to speak up is regarded as dangerous and subversive; how does she expect to find a place for herself and her students here, "where people have been gazing at their navels for the past twenty years?" Angrily reciting a litany of Italian stereotypes encountered in Montreal, he scornfully suggests that Italians' recent "notoriety" has in fact made little difference to the immigrant community:

> After having been job-stealers, strangers, Wops, mafiosi, spaghetti, the others and the ethnics, now we're the allophones. Have you ever heard an uglier term? That should be the registered trademark of some phone! (66-67).

In *Addolorata* (1984), Micone turns to the second generation of Italian immigrants, examining the power relationships between father/daughter and husband/wife and the struggle to retain/reject the traditional role of male authoritarianism. The common link in both plays is the powerlessness of the immigrant, both male and female, torn between the contradictory demands of the culture of the Italian village and that of the Montreal metropolis. Awarded the Grand Prix de théâtre du Journal de Montreal (1989) for *Déjà l'agonie* [*Beyond the Ruins*], Micone turns to prose in *Le Figuier enchanté* (1992) [The Enchanted Fig Tree], an unusual amalgam of biography, fiction and theatre in which he traces his father's departure from La Molise in Italy and his own, some years later, as a young boy. On a subsequent return to visit his Italian relatives, Micone rushes off to see the "magic fig tree" of his childhood, only to find, to his astonishment, that his grandfather has grafted a different variety onto the original one, resulting in a magnificent hybrid laden with purple figs clustered beside huge green ones.

Micone, in his closing chapter, is perhaps the first Quebec writer to offer stereotypes of Francophone Québécois as perceived by Allophones living in Montreal. Choosing as decor an imaginary conversation between two women, he juxtaposes a "typical" Francophone mother of a family, Anna, who expresses her annoyance at the attitudes of immigrants, and the feisty Manuela, a highly qualified teacher who speaks four languages but whose certification has not been recognized by the Ministry of Education. Anna's expression of fear that French will ultimately disappear in Quebec is met with ironic disdain as Manuela reassures her this cannot possibly happen because her own children no longer understand their grandparents, because French and not Italian is the language her children now speak. With biting sarcasm she begs Anna forgiveness because immigrants from her country have "stolen" jobs that French Canadians didn't want, for moving into districts already abandoned by Francophones, for being able to work as a seamstress at minimum wage all day long, and above all, for not knowing about Bill 101 and the Charter of the French Language, before arriving in Montreal.

In another chapter, Micone's sensitivity to the beauty of the spoken word is apparent as he recalls, fondly, the poems his father would compose and recite in Molisan dialect on returning every night from the drudgery of the factory:

> Ces mots sont ceux de mon enfance. Tant qu'ils évoqueront un monde que les mots d'ici ne pourront saisir, je resterai un immigrant par une double nostalgie (99).
>
> [These words are those of my childhood. As long as they conjure up a world that words from this place cannot express, I shall remain an immigrant because I am doubly nostalgic.]

Without hesitation or apology, Micone describes his twofold sense of belonging: "Ni tout à fait italienne, ni tout à fait québécoise, ma culture est métissée" (100). [Neither entirely Italian, nor entirely Québécoise, my culture is a hybrid mix.] One of a new breed within the Italian community of Montreal, he has chosen French, rather than English, as the language of choice. At the same time, he is determined not to reject his cultural heritage nor to assimilate into a French majority. Just as the "magic fig tree" through grafting became more productive and beautiful, so too, suggests Micone, will the culture of the immigrant, a transitional culture at best, enrich and make more fruitful than ever before the culture of Quebec.

In 1978 Dany Laferrière left Haiti, a political exile, to eke out a living in Montreal, tanning cowhides in a local factory. Eight years later, he published his first novel, *Comment faire l'amour à un nègre sans se fatiguer* (1985) which became an instant best-seller, was translated (by David Homel) into English [*How to Make Love to a Negro*] (1987) and then adapted for a film version (1989) that, in Paris, attracted a much greater attendance than *Jesus de Montréal.* The story line revolves around the exotic adventures of two individuals, the anonymous narrator trying to produce a first novel in the style of Henry Miller and Bouba, a Cartesian rationalist who sits on his couch facing Mecca, reads the Koran twice a day and proudly admits that "Allah est grand et Freud est son prophète" [Allah is great and Freud is his prophet]. Living in a stuffy, run-down apartment at 3670 rue Saint-Denis, the two intellectuals attract a constant stream of liberated young women from McGill, eager to discuss philosophy and jazz with Bouba, the guru, and to experience the culture of the Black, primarily through sex. As the narrator explains, in one of his many monologues, "Baiser nègre, c'est baiser autrement! [To screw black-man style is to screw in a very different way!]

Social gaffes often mark the narrator's first contacts with the wealthy Anglophone world: visiting the luxurious apartment of Miz Chat, the proud owner of prize-winners Lady Barbarella d'Odessa and Blue Salvador Nasseau, and seeking to impress, he makes the fatal error of telling his host about the quaint custom in his country of eating cats as a daily staple. His favourite companion, Miz Littérature, currently writing a thesis on Christine de Pisan, is intent on freeing him from a down-trodden past by feeding him exquisite Oka cheese, pâté de foie gras, Greek desserts and imported wines. Laferrière's novel is marked by humor and forthright eroticism, appealing to the Quebec intellectual by specific references to Conquest by white oppressors (always English!) and to writers and singers such as Carole Laure currently in vogue in Montreal. The underlying tenor, despite its apparent flippancy, is profoundly serious, as suggested by the allusion to Article One of the *Code noir* [Black Code] (1685) which defines the Black man as "a piece of furniture". Laferrière's originality is evident at many levels; his ironic description of Carré St. Louis, the fiefdom of such Quebec legends as Emile Nelligan, Pauline Julien and Michel Tremblay, as a hangout for unsavoury drunks and his passing reference to the (Islamic) crescent moon shining above the Christian cross of Mount Royal suggest that the fictional landscape of Montreal has been changed by startling new images and voices from a Francophone culture that, although French, is definitely not Québécois.

Sex, atomic bombs and sushi form the core of a second novel, *Eroshima* (1987); in the 1990s, however, Laferrière wrote six more books, all dealing with Haitians and all of which made the best-seller lists. His departure for Miami before the arrival of winter in 1990 put him back in touch with his Haitian roots. In *L'Odeur du café* (1991) [*An Aroma of Coffee*] he travels back to the tiny village of Petit-Goâve in 1963, a time of intense happiness in his life, when his grandmother, Da, protected him with love and tenderness from the outside world of the Duvalier regime. *Le Goût des jeune filles* (1992) [*Dining with the Dictator*] moves on to 1971, describing a weekend in the life of a teenager in Port-au-Prince. Structured in the manner of a film, with few long descriptions but much dialogue, this novel reflects the matriarchal upbringing of its author: the few male characters fade into the background as Laferrière paints vibrant, intense sketches of women of all ages. The "jeunes filles" of the title refer to his good friends, the "boarders" living with Miki, and turn out to be young girls his own age who, despite their sordid life as prostitutes, exhibit in Dany's presence an uninhibited sense of freshness and innocence.

The third novel in Laferrière's Haitian cycle documents the arrival of a 23 year-old who gets off the boat in Montreal and one day becomes a writer. *Chronique de la dérive douce* (1994) [*A Year Adrift*], with its 365 fragments of a few short lines set in 1976, represents an attempt by the author to experiment in form; it is also a variant of his first novel; this time, however, the milieu and names are Francophone. The traumatic solitude of the immigrant provides the essential core of the narrative, as the protagonist, from a socially prominent family and surrounded by friends, finds himself suddenly in a city where he is "nothing more than a Black." Laferrière's first trip back to Haiti provides the matter for *Pays sans chapeau* (1996), [*Down Among the Dead Men (1997)*] a series of sketches in which he explores long-forgotten facets of a previous life. Warned by his mother that Port-au-Prince is filled by people "without hats", a cemetery filled with the living dead, he comes up against superstition and voodoo, as well as the affection of elderly aunts who invite him to kneel for prayer, as they did when he was a little boy. *La Chair du maître* (1997) once again relies on short episodes, consisting for the most part of lively dialogue and large numbers of characters who appear and disappear, such as Prophète, the Voodoo priest and painter. Sex, politics, and poverty buffet the reader, but for the first time in Laferrière's brief career, with little humor and disturbing violence inflicted by "the new masters of the poor."

Unlike Laferrière's fascination with the recent past, Paul Ohl, Alsatian by birth and immigrant to Canada in 1951 at age eleven, turns his attention to ancient civilizations. First learning the craft of writing in books about the heritage of the Samurai and critiques of systemic exploitation in the commercial boxing world, in 1987, he published *Katana: le roman du*

Japon [Katana: Novel of Japan], an authentic fictional recreation of seventeenth century Japan which reflects his personal interest in the martial arts and the science of war, as well as his admiration of the philosophical values of the feudal Shogunate. Providing an excellent glossary and a brief historical overview, Ohl counterbalances the violence of warfare brought about in part by the newly arrived presence of Christianity with the cultural sensitivity of Samurai who are as skillful with the flute as they are with the traditional sword. In an epilogue, aptly entitled "The Twilight of Humanity," we move to 1945 where he narrates the last morning in the life of a young aviator who visits the Temple of the Great Buddha, before flying off on a kamikaze mission, offering his life freely to the Emperor, in the finest tradition of the Samurai. Carrying the ancient sword of a family ancestor into his cockpit, Naoki flies off, at 11:00 am on August 9, to be annihilated over Nagasaki by an atomic bomb.

Ohl's talents are even more evident in *Drakkar: le roman des Vikings* (1989) [Drakkar: Novel of the Vikings] where he skillfully juxtaposes the Christian beliefs of medieval Europe with those of pagan Scandinavia in the year 1100. Raiding expeditions as far away as Rouen where churches were burned and monks were kidnapped because they could read and write provide the expected blood and gore. However, once back in Iceland, a colony of Norwegian Vikings, we witness the lesser known qualities of a conquering people: their skills in building the fragile *drakkars* and navigating in unknown waters, their fierce attachment to their democratic Parliament and the rich literary heritage of saga and verse recited by their bards. Ohl thus redresses the stereotyped violence of the American film, *The Vikings* (1958), starring Kirk Douglas, which had first sparked his interest in this people. Lyrical and at times poetic, *Drakkar* is a fitting homage to the people of Iceland and to Halldor Kiljan Laxness who won the Nobel Prize for literature in 1955.

Ohl's most powerful and complex novel, *Soleil noir: le roman de la Conquête* (1991) [Black Sun: Novel of the Conquest], focuses on sixteenth century Bolivia and Peru, alternating between November 1532, when the last Inca was taken hostage by the Spaniards, and July 1989, when a freelance collector of antique artifacts, Vadim Herzog, arrives in search of the death mask of Atahualpa, the last king of the Incas who was put to death by Francisco Pizarro. His cynicism turns to compassion when he is led through the jungle to the mine at Potosi, described by his guides as "the gateway to hell, the greatest tomb in the world" where incredible numbers of workers have been exploited and died since the Spanish Conquest. One of Ohl's most fascinating and complex characters is Santiago Vilca, a revolutionary priest and musician, who leads Herzog back through history, revealing all the horrors of occupation by the Spaniards, their rape of the country, their theft of gold and silver, their successful attempts at annihilation and the magnificent beliefs of his ancestors, the Incas.

A fourth novel, *L'Enfant dragon* (1994) [The Dragon Child], is set in Canton, China, in the 1920s where a Scottish paleontologist and his Canadian wife, in defending the merits of Chinese culture, criticize Western influences and British occupation. Though perhaps less gripping than *Soleil noir*, it follows the pattern of powerful descriptions, well-constructed plots, elegant language and reveals the author's continuing admiration of, and sensitivity to, other cultures. Ohl's careful research of his topic, always balanced by a lengthy stay in the geographical setting of his plot, and his sense of the sweep of history, have given new life to the historical novel in Quebec, and provided a distinctive North American Francophone parallel to Clavell and Michener.

In 1989, Ying Chen, a young woman born in Shanghai in 1961, moved to McGill University where she had been accepted in a program of creative writing: between 1992 and 1995 she produced, in French, three successful novels in which she explores the weight of tradition within the Chinese family, and writes about the pain of exile separating two young people in love. In *La Mémoire de l'eau* (1992) [Memory of Water] we relive sixty years of Chinese history through the eyes of Grandmother Lie-Fei, born just before the fall of the last Chinese emperor in 1912. Lie-Fei tries to comprehend the startling changes that sweep through her country and affect her personal life as she moves from childhood to old age. As a little girl, custom demanded that her feet be bound to make them "as beautiful as lotus flowers," but with the approval of her enlightened father, she removes the bindings, leaving her with feet too large compared to traditional bound feet and too small compared to normal ones. This decision will have serious consequences for Lie-Fei, because the reaction of the public to her strange-looking appearance will provoke contradictory reactions, depending on the political ideology currently in favor. At one point, she is seen as a victim of feudalistic custom; at another, she is reproached for choosing to have "feudal feet." Though her narrative ends shortly after the Cultural Revolution with a flight to New York, Chen omits specific criticism of political events, such as the Tienanmen Massacre, preferring to analyze the minutiae of daily living and observe with respectful compassion the necessary adaptations people such as her grandmother must constantly make to the contradictory winds of change. As the narrator suggests:

> Les modes changent avec le temps, alors que les hommes (et les femmes) demeurent les mêmes, comme ces lotus qui, par nécessité, s'installent éternellement dans la boue en dépit de l'eau qui coule sans cesse.
>
> [Fashions change with the times, while men (and women) remain the same, like the lotus flowers which, by necessity, sink their roots ever more deeply into the muddy bottom despite the incessantly changing currents that flow past.]

In her first novel, Chen prefers to pay discreet and tender homage to a elderly woman who has survived only by learning the lesson of the lotus flower.

In *Les Lettres chinoises* (1993) [Chinese Letters] Chen chooses the form of the epistolary novel, in which Yuan announces to his beloved Sassa that he has decided to leave Shanghai and settle in Montreal. In an exchange of letters, the young couple tries to nourish their mutual affection but distance and differing attitudes exacerbate their physical separation. For Yuan, exile is a necessary migration, though not necessarily painful, his model being

> ces oiseaux qui voyagent à travers le temps et l'espace, construisant partout leurs nids pour chanter leurs chansons (53).
>
> [the birds which travel through time and space, building their nests everywhere in order to sing their songs.]

Sassa however is terrified by the very thought:

> Je crains de devenir trop visible dans un autre pays. C'est affreux de vivre sous les regards quand on a déjà perdu toute fierté pour sa propre image et son propre pays. Et s'il faut mourir, il vaut mieux que ce soit dans les ténèbres tranquilles que dans les lumières curieuses.

> [I am afraid of becoming too visible in another country. It is frightening to live with people watching you when you have already lost all pride in your self image and of your own country. And if one must die, it is better this happen in peaceful shadows than in the glare of unknown lights.]

Chen suggests obliquely in an interview that the crushing weight of Chinese traditions had at least some bearing in her own move to Montreal, though her choice of Quebec satisfied a double interest in her life, that of America and France. *Les Lettres chinoises* reveal, frequently with discreet irony, the pain that accompanies such a difficult choice.

In *L'Ingratitude* (1995) [Ingratitude] set in post-Mao China, a young woman who has experienced the 1968 Revolution, balks at the strictures and lack of privacy imposed by village life, where family, work and political orthodoxy regiment the daily life of every individual. The female narrator aims her revolt, not at a beloved grandmother but at her autocratic mother, who constantly badgers her to conform to traditional ways of thinking, acting and making choices. What is extraordinary about Yan-Zi's revolt and resentment is that her carefully formulated plan to take her own life by an overdose of pills has gone awry; instead, she has been struck down by a passing vehicle. It is while awaiting imminent death on a hospital bed that she expresses all this, smelling the black smoke of the crematorium, seeing the burial of her ashes in the cemetery and observing her mother returning home for the final ceremonial tea, relieved that rumours of a suicide attempt, the ultimate social disgrace, have been put to rest by this tragedy. Death, for Yan-Zi, turns out to be the only escape possible from maternal tyranny; it also represents a step into the limbo of nothingness.

In 1994, another first novelist, this time a fifty-year old Brazilian fluent in German and Portuguese, Sergio Kokis, took Montreal's critics by storm, *Le Pavillon des miroirs* [The House of Mirrors] winning four of Quebec's five major literary prizes: the Grand Prix du livre de Montreal, the Prix de l'Académie des lettres du Québec, the Prix France-Quebec and the Prix Desjardins du roman du Salon du livre du Québec. In chapters alternating between the vivid memories and images of childhood in Rio and the reflections of an adult experiencing the cold winter landscape of Quebec, Kokis recreates the first twenty years or so of the narrator-painter who, inspired by the colors and forms of his Brazilian youth, tries to integrate them into his canvases. Insisting that his novel is not autobiographical, he prefers to see it as an exploration of art and creativity, an opinion confirmed on many pages of this book, including the narrator's striking description of the art of the painter as "des jeux de miroir, un colin-maillard avec des ombres et des reflets" [tricks of the mirror, a game of blind man's buff with shadows and reflections]. In the sole allusion to contemporary Quebec, the narrator-traveller explains what so attracted him to this place: the tradition of pioneers, hunters and *coureurs de bois* he had read about in books, types such as Bethune and Tom Thomson, at home and at peace with the great wilderness of the Northern landscape. In his 25 year quest, he has found no trace whatsoever of these mythical figures of song and legend, invented perhaps by clerics who have now been replaced by the new priests of culture, by "curés en civil" [priests in laymen's clothes] and matrons on television and in the press, counseling us on what to believe, about what we should wear and how we should act. People here, he has discovered, are no different from those in the land he has left behind: aboriginals on welfare and drunks on the street are as wretched as the dispossessed in the *favelas* of his youth.

In the final chapter of this novel, the narrator describes the specific stages each immigrant must undergo: the arrival in an unknown city, where the sun shines less brightly than at home; the close observation of the crowds passing in the streets in order "to capture the laws of their specific hive of activity"; the anguish and trauma of the first nights spent alone. In conclusion, he summarizes the essential nature of the foreigner in exile:

> Ce déraciné oscille ainsi entre deux temps, le sien et le réel, en arrière et en avant, sans pouvoir se fixer ... L'étranger ne peut pas toujours se détacher vers l'avenir: il est souvent embourbé entre cette identité qui fut et la béance de devoir devenir autre ... Cette nostalgie d'un passé qu'on n'ose pas affronter amène l'étranger à l'embellir, à le refaire dans sa tête. Il se déguise et se fige dans un mouvement de pendule entre le plus-que-parfait et le futur antérieur (360-61).
>
> [This rootless person wavers between two times, his own and the real one, backwards and forwards, without being able to situate himself ... The foreigner can't always become detached with an eye on the future: he is frequently caught between the identity that once was and the obligation to become something else ... This nostalgia for a past one dares not confront leads the outsider to embellish it, to make it over in his head. He disguises himself and gets stuck in the movement of a pendulum swinging back and forth between the pluperfect and the future anterior.]

In his second novel, *Negão et Doralice* (1995), Kokis returns to South America, conjuring up exuberantly the sights and sounds of the Brazil of his childhood and plunging his readers into the poverty of the Third World. Against the 1972 backdrop of the slums and red-light districts of Rio, during the week preceding Carnival, Kokis explores with shocking objectivity the sordid life of the city's underbelly. The thirty year old mulatto, Negão, a dock worker and thief specializing in the stealing of luxury cars, kills three policemen to prevent them raping his lover, Doralice, an 18 year old red-headed whore. He is pursued throughout the novel by Dr. Vigario, a political officer of the current dictatorship in a manhunt on the eve of Carnival that recalls at times the mood and setting of Marcel Camus's *Orfeo negro* [*Black Orpheus*] and ends with the gang-rape by police of Doralice and the vengeful torture of her defender. Partly detective story, partly a critique of the dictatorial violence that crushes the destitute, it introduces the reader to the milieu in which Kokis was raised as a child, a harsh but exotic world where magic and myth are as important as reality and where love may blossom, even in the depths of brutality and oppression.

Kokis chooses East Berlin in 1986 as the setting for *Errances* (1996) [Wanderings] where Boris Nikto, a Brazilian poet who has lived in exile for 22 years after escaping a military coup, has been granted an amnesty and invitation to return to his native land. In a successful juxtaposition of a past filled with images of violence and a present filled with self doubts and unease, the author sketches vividly and convincingly the surprise and confusion overwhelming his narrator as he leaves Iron Curtain territory to return to the democratic milieu of Bremen where West German intellectuals welcome him as a hero and model for the young. Though ponderous at times, Kokis's vast erudition and distaste for academic pedantry is also amusing, particularly when, during a special conference devoted entirely to his writings, professors using the technical jargon of marxism, structuralism and semiotics, proudly reveal how their theories have uncovered unique insights into their guest's poetry of exile and which the dismayed Nikto realizes have no relationship whatsoever to what he has written. The Brazilian consul in East Berlin promises Nikto a safe welcome home on his return to Rio, because the new regime is forgetting the past and "starting all over from zero." The poet's illusions are soon shattered, as he finds that his revolutionary comrades of the 1960s have now embraced the luxury and privilege of a new middle class, and Clarissa, the passionate rebel whose features he had constantly sought to recapture in the body of every woman he subsequently met, had married soon after his hasty departure from the country, has recently divorced, and now embraces fully the conservative, materialistic values of the new ruling class. Nikto soon discovers the emptiness of the consul's promise: desertion within the officer class is still the unforgivable sin; once again, he must find false identity papers and flee the country to avoid arrest and imprisonment. Cerebral and sensual, *Errances* is both a fascinating study of exile and a disturbing questioning of the nature of reality which the writer attempts to shape and form through the written word. It also confirms his ease with the structures of fiction and the elegance of his prose, even if the story line is often swept aside by the flood of ideas expressing the author's probing reflections on life.

Montreal critics have welcomed the wave of new writers from other cultural backgrounds, referring to them as "Néo-Québécois" and creators of "the other Québécois literature." Despite the good intentions of its users, the terminology suggests a sub-text: that these authors are in the process of becoming "one of us"--- but not yet. Similarly, the suggestion that writing by, for example, such diverse individuals as Micone, Laferrière, Chen and Kokis (Ohl rarely being defined as "culturally different"), may be categorized by a single homogenous grouping is somewhat unsettling.

What has happened in the last four decades is that Quebec fiction has moved from stereotypes about immigrants and outsiders to writers who are "immigrants" to the most recent plateau of "immigrants as writers." This latter group of ambitious authors are probing, in time or in space, the psyche of other cultures and re-drawing (to use the felicitous phrase of Eli Mandel) "the psychological landscape of the immigrant." It would appear that the grafting of Micone's "magic fig tree" has started to bear rich fruit on a trunk that is already mature and vigorous, as these "voices from elsewhere" speak about "elsewhere."

Works Cited and Bibliography

Chen, Ying. *La Mémoire de l'eau.* Montreal: Léméac, 1992.

_____. *Les Lettres chinoises.* Montreal: Léméac, 1995.

_____. *L'Ingratitude.* Montreal: Léméac, 1993.

Hathorn, Ramon. "L'Irlandais dans le roman québécois." *Etudes Irlandaises* (Lille III) (December 1977), 117-23.

_____. "L'Appel de la race: la Colette Baudoche du Canada français." *Solitude rompue,* R. Robidoux and C. Cloutier, Editors. Ottawa: Editions de l'université d'Ottawa, 1986, 150-55.

_____. "Lionel-Adolphe Groulx," "Sergio Kokis," "Paul Ohl." *The Oxford Companion to Canadian Literature,* second edition. Edited by E. Benson and W. Toye. Toronto: Oxford University Press, 1997.

Jonaissant, Jean. "Autoportraits de l'autre littérature québécoise." *Lettres québécoises* (été 1992), 1-16.

Kokis, Sergio. *Le Pavillon des miroirs.* Montreal: XYZ, 1994.

_____. *Negão et Doralice.* Montreal: XYZ, 1995.

_____. *Errances.* Montreal: XYZ , 1996.

Laferrière, Dany. *Comment faire l'amour à un nègre sans se fatiquer.* Montreal: VLB Editeur, 1985. [*How to make love to a Negro.*] Translated by David Homel. Toronto: Coach House Press, 1987.

_____. *Eroshima.* Montreal: VLB Editeur, 1987. [*Eroshima].* Translated by David Homel. Toronto: Coach House Press, 1991.

_____. *L'Odeur du café.* Montreal: VLB Editeur, 1991. [*An Aroma of Coffee]* Translated by David Homel. Toronto: Coach House Press, 1993.

_____. *Le Goût des jeunes filles.* Montreal : VLB Editeur, 1992. *[Dining with the dictator.]* Translated by David Homel. Toronto: Coach House Press, 1994.

_____. *Cette Grenade dans la main du jeune Nègre est-elle une arme ou un fruit?* Montreal: VLB Editeur, 1993. [*Why must a black writer write about sex?]* Translated by David Homel. Toronto: Coach House Press, 1994.

_____. *Chronique de la dérive douce.* Montreal: VLB Editeur, 1994. [*A Drifting* Year.] Translated by David Homel. Toronto: Douglas & McIntyre, 1997

_____. *Pays sans chapeau.* Montreal: Lanctôt Editeur, 1996. [*Down Among the Dead Men.]* Translated by David Homel. Toronto: Douglas & McIntyre.

_____. *La Chair du maître.* Montreal: Lanctôt Editeur, 1997.

Linteau, Paul-André. " Montréal". *The Canadian Encyclopedia III.* Edmonton: Hurtig Publishers, 1988, 1379-83.

Mandel, Eli. "Ethnic Voice in Canadian Writing". *Another time.* Erin, Ontario: Press Porcepic, 1977.

_____. *Contexts of Canadian Criticism.* Chicago: University of Chicago Press, 1971.

Micone, Marco. *Gens du silence.* Montreal: Québec/Amérique, 1982. *[Voiceless People.]* Translated by Maurizia Binda. Montreal: Guernica, 1984.

_____. *Addolorata.* Montreal: Editions Guernica, 1984. (Two Plays. *Voiceless People, Addolorata.)* Translated by Maurizia Binda. Montreal , Guernica, 1991.

_____. *Déjà l'agonie.* Montreal: Boréal, 1993.

Ohl, Paul, *Katana: le roman du Japon.* Montreal: Editions Québec/Amérique, 1987.

_____. *Drakkar: le roman des Vikings.* Montréal: Editions Québec/Amérique, 1989.

_____. *Soleil noir: le roman de la Conquête.* Montreal: Editions Québec/Amérique, 1991.

_____. *L'Enfant dragon.* Montreal: Libre Expression, 1994.

Ollivier, Emile. *Paysage de l'aveugle.* Montreal: Editions Pierre Tisseyre, 1977.

_____. *Haïti, quel développement?* (essai en collaboration). Montreal: Collectif paroles, 1978.

_____. *Mère-solitude.* Paris: Albin Michel, 1983.

_____. *La Discorde aux cent voix.* Paris: Albin Michel, 1986.

_____. *Passages.* Montreal: L'Hexagone, 1991.

Tremblay, Michael. *A toi pour toujours ta Marie-Lou.* Montreal: Léméac, 1973. [*Forever yours, Marie-Lou.*] Translated by John Van Burek and Bill Glassco. Vancouver, B.C.: Talonbooks, 1974.

Additional Reading:

Simon, Sherry. "The Language of Difference: Minority Writers in Quebec." *A/Part. Papers from the 1984 Ottowa Conference on Language, Culture and Literary Identity in Canada.* Edited by J.U. Bumsted. *Canadian Litrature, Supplement No.1,* 1987, 119-128.

Mothers and Daughters in Contemporary Quebec Fiction

Susan Ireland
Grinnell College, Iowa

The loss of the daughter to the mother, the mother to the daughter, is the essential female tragedy. Adrienne Rich, *Of Woman Born: Motherhood as Experience and Institution*, 237.

Le rapport mère-fille est le *continent noir* du *continent noir*, c'est ce qu'il y a de plus obscur dans notre culture actuelle. Luce Irigarary, *Le Corps- à-corps*, 61. [The mother-daughter relationship is *the dark continent* of *the dark continent*. It is the most obscure part of our culture today.]

In her seminal work, *Of Woman Born* (1976), Adrienne Rich observes that the "cathexis between mother and daughter . . . is the great unwritten story" (225). Five years later, Luce Irigaray again stresses the importance of refiguring the mother-daughter relationship: "La relation mère/fille, fille/mère constitue un noyau extrêmement explosif dans nos sociétés. La penser, la changer, revient à ébranler l'ordre patriarcal" (Irigarary 1981, 86). [The mother/daughter, daughter/mother relationship is a highly explosive nucleus in society today. Conceptualizing it, changing it, amounts to destabilizing the patriarchal system.] Irigaray emphasizes the destructive nature of matricidal Western cultures and holds them responsible for damaging the relations between mother and daughter by suppressing the mother's voice and occulting female genealogies.[1] As the "sous-sol muet" [the silent foundation] of the social order (Irigaray 1981, 81), however, mothers and daughters (future mothers) form the foundation on which the entire system is built, a foundation that could bring down the whole patriarchal house if it were destabilized --- "si nous faisons bouger le fondement de l'ordre social, tout bouge" (Irigaray 1981, 81). [If we destabilize the foundation of the social order, the whole structure moves.] For this reason, writing the mother-daughter story, and thereby putting an end to the silence surrounding it, forms a central part of the feminist project.

The first stage of the feminist engagement with the mother-daughter story is represented by the fictional and theoretical works of the 1960s and early 1970s that focus primarily on the perspective of the daughter and equate motherhood with servitude. In these daughter-centered texts, motherhood is generally presented as incompatible with self-fulfillment, and the mother embodies the role the daughter wishes to reject: "the mother stands for the victim in ourselves, the unfree woman, the martyr" (Rich 236). This mother-daughter, enslavement-freedom dichotomy led many feminists to distinguish between mothers and non-mothers and to suggest that women must opt for one or the other --- "sois 'femme-libre-célibataire,' ou 'mère attachée'" (LaRue 53). [Be either a 'free-unmarried-woman' or 'an enshackled mother.'] Consequently, many texts written during this period are characterized by their "matrophobia," the daughter's fear of becoming her mother,[2] and suggest that liberating oneself from the cycle of servitude entails what Rich calls a form of "radical surgery" --- severing one's ties with the mother (236).

The emphasis on the daughter has led critics such as Marianne Hirsch to call for a change in focus and for a greater emphasis on the perspective of the mother: "I am asking not only where the stories of women are in men's plots but where the stories of mothers are in the plots of sons and daughters" (Hirsch 4). In a similar vein, writers such as LaRue have questioned the distinction between mothers and other women, thus implicitly accusing feminism of perpetuating the matricidal tendencies of Western culture: "Mais, l'amour des femmes, que devrait nommer le mot féminisme, ne devra-t-il pas tôt ou tard inclure l'amour et la pensée de la mère *réelle*?" (LaRue 54). [But surely love of women --- which the term feminism should designate --- will sooner or later have to include love for and the thoughts of real mothers?] As if in response to these protests, the second stage of the mother-daughter story, which began in the mid 1970s, has seen a shift from the earlier matrophobia to "a courageously sustained quest for the mother" (Showalter 1986, 135). During this period, theorists such as Nancy Chodorow, Elisabeth Badinter, Ann Dally, Julia Kristeva, Hélène Cixous, and Irigaray have examined the institution of motherhood and its effects on women from a variety of perspectives --- social, cultural, literary, and psychological.[3] In the context of Qubec, Karen Gould argues that this search for the mother "may well be one of the most significant developments in Quebec fiction of the last decade" (114). Although the daughter's perspective was at first the main focus of feminist works published in Quebec, as it was in many other countries,[4] in the 1980s, the mother appears as "a subject of exploration rather than as an object of resentment, repression and narrative silence" (Gould 114).[5] Monique LaRue's mother-centered texts, for example, address a wide range of issues related to motherhood and maternity, and urge women to abandon the opposition between motherhood and feminism, reproduction and creativity. Writers of this period thus recognize the importance of reassessing motherhood, and acknowledge that the repression of the mother by earlier feminists is a question that must be addressed. As LaRue puts it, "Le problème avec la mère, aujourd'hui, demeure: *qu'en faire?* Car où qu'on la fuie, dénie, refoule, elle revient" (LaRue 52). [The problem with the mother today is still: what should we do with her? For however we try to run away from her, to disclaim her, to repress her, we can't get away from her.]

As the mother-daughter story moves into its next stage, the emphasis is on reconciliation and moving forward together. This reconciliation involves creating mother-daughter relationships that are no longer matricidal on either the personal or the societal levels. For the individual, this means reconciling women's roles as mother *and* woman --- "nous n'avons pas à renoncer à être des femmes pour être des mères" (Irigaray 1981, 27) [we shouldn't have to give up being women in order to be mothers] --- while in a broader context developing new models of mother-daughter relations based on mutual support, "un rapport réciproque de femme à femme" (Irigaray 86) [a reciprocal woman-to-woman relationship] that allows mothers and daughters to work together to bring about change. Rather than liberating one pole of the relationship from the other, the goal now, as Irigaray argues, is to "nous libérer *avec* nos mères" (86, my emphasis) [to liberate ourselves *along with* our mothers.] As part of this trend, a series of texts published in the late 1980s and the 1990s suggests a move from the matrophobia of the earlier daughter-centered works to a reconciliation with the mother. In Quebec, these recent texts include a significant number written by women of immigrant descent, and the renewed interest in the mother-daughter question thus coincides with the emergence of a substantial body of ethnic literature, otherwise known as "l'écriture migrante."[6] These women writers seek both to undermine the foundations of the patriarchal order and to find a place for themselves within Quebec culture and the traditional canon of Quebec literature. This essay will examine the notion of reconciliation in the work of four women of immigrant descent --- Tiziana Beccarelli Saad, Bianca Zagolin, Ying Chen, and Nadia Ghalem. In particular, it will look at the different historical events and personal itineraries that shape the mother-daughter relationship and will focus on the interrelated themes of exile, voice, madness and suicide used to characterize that relationship.

In Beccarelli Saad's *Vers l'Amérique*, [Towards America] the relations between four generations of mothers and daughters are played out against the backdrop of two World Wars and between the geographical poles of Italy and North America. The presentation of several generations enables Beccarelli Saad to portray several of the women as both daughters and mothers, and to engage in the kind of genealogical exploration Irigaray deems necessary "pour ne pas être complices du meurtre de la mère" (Irigaray 1981, 29)[7] [if we are not to become accomplices of matricide]. Between the two stories of emigration recounted in the novel --- one marked by failure and the other representing hope for the future --- the dominant emotions in the mother-daughter relationship evolve from resentment and powerlessness to understanding and control.

The relationship between the first two generations, those of Teresa and her mother, is determined by the constraints of class and gender in an Italian village at the turn of the century. Teresa's mother, powerless and voiceless in her role as reproducer, represents the "sous-sol muet" (Irigaray 1981, 81) [silent foundation] and occupies an inferior position in the Father's House.[8] Shaped by traditional patriarchal values, she values her sons over her daughters and thus plays a role in perpetuating male-defined familial and societal structures: "la vieille avait appris à ne compter que sur ses fils, ses hommes, et elle n'avait que mépris pour les 'créatures.' Ses propres filles n'y échappaient pas" (Saad 12-13) [the old lady had learned to count only on her sons, her men, and she had only scorn for 'creatures.' Her own daughters were no exception.] Doubly disadvantaged as a woman and a member of a poor rural family, her daughter Teresa is "une de celles destinées à être traitées en inférieures" (Saad 14) [someone destined to be treated as inferior], just as her mother was. Because of her mother's silence and apparent complicity with the status quo, Teresa's attitude towards her mother is one of resentment: "Teresa supportait de plus en plus difficilement l'indifférence de la vieille à son égard" (Saad 12). [Teresa found it increasingly difficult to put up with the old lady's indifference towards her.]

Although Teresa leaves her father's house at the age of fifteen, she moves from one form of subjection to another. Sent by her father to live with her brother in America, she has no control over her own destiny --- "son sort est réglé, elle n'a rien à dire" (Saad 13) [her fate is sealed, she has no say in it] --- and emigration brings no liberation from the constraints of either class or gender. In New York, she works twelve hours a day in an exploitative job making artificial flowers, while her brother replaces her father as the figure of authority, his role reinforced by the voice of the Church --- "Et Dieu dit que l'homme commande à la femme" (Saad 17) [And God said that man rules over woman]. Teresa thus remains silent and disempowered, her psychological alienation reflecting her physical exile, and her failure to learn English symbolizing her lack of voice. At this point in the novel, her main fear is that she will unwillingly perpetuate the cycle of victimization by becoming her mother: "Teresa ne connaît que le silence. Personne ne lui a appris d'autres mots que ceux qui parlent labeur, souffrance, chagrin. Teresa devient comme la vieille. Il fallait donc qu'elle parte si loin pour lui ressembler, après tout" (Saad 24). [Teresa knows only silence. Nobody has taught her any words other than those that speak of work, suffering, and sorrow. Teresa is becoming like her old lady. Had she had to travel so far, then, only to resemble her after all.]

After her brother's death, Teresa's new job caring for three children brings her into contact with a more privileged social group and a different type of mother figure, and marks the beginning of her emancipation. With an educated woman ("Madame") rather than a working-class man as the primary influence in her life, Teresa learns the conditions needed to control one's own destiny: a voice and the ability to "se faire respecter" (Saad 31) [earn respect]. Consequently, when she returns to live in Italy, she resolves to change the gender relations of her childhood by earning the respect of the men in the village --- "Ils ne l'auront pas! . . . Elle gagnera le respect de ces fils d'hommes têtus et ignorants" (Saad 14). [They won't get her. She will win the respect of these sons of obstinate, ignorant men.][9] Although she fails to make a new life for herself in New York, America nonetheless serves as a symbol of potential change and, as such, stands in opposition to the traditional patriarchal values of the village.[10] Teresa's change in perspective is underscored by her symbolic purchase of "la maison paternelle" (Saad 11) [the father's house], and her position as proprietor of "SA maison" (Saad 13) [HER house] provides a sharp contrast to her mother's position in the same house.

Running her own House --- forging her destiny within the confines of a patriarchal society --- brings Teresa into conflict with the men of her family, who symbolically want to take over her house. This unwanted intrusion crystallizes her feelings of anger: "Il lui vient des rages folles de n'être pas un homme . . . Folie, folie de penser qu'une femme, même avec un peu de biens, peut s'en sortir seule" (Saad 31).

[She is given to violent rage at not being a man. Folly, what folly to think that a woman can make it on her own, even when she has a little property.] At the same time, she expresses frustration with the local women who, like her own mother, show no sign of revolt when humiliated by their husbands --- "toutes ces pauvresses autour d'elle qui acceptent n'importe quoi, n'importe quoi, venant de leurs maris" (Saad 31) [all those poor wretches who accept everything, absolutely everything, from their husbands]. Rather than capitulate entirely --- a surrender that would return her to the same position as her mother --- Teresa seeks a compromise that enables her to maintain control of her House: as a solution, she proposes marriage to Amedeo, one of the more silent men in the village. The decision to marry and the difficulty of changing traditional attitudes bring Teresa to a new understanding of her mother in which the earlier resentment gives way to compassion and reconciliation: "peut-être que sa vieille avait souffert de sa condition et qu'il pouvait lui être consolant de constater qu'au moins un de ses enfants était parvenu là où elle avait voulu se hausser. La lourde hérédité de la pauvreté venait, à l'instant même, dans la tête de Teresa de mourir" (Saad 14). [Maybe her old lady had suffered because of her situation and would be comforted to know that at least one of her children had managed to improve her lot in the way she would have liked to have done herself. At that very moment, the heavy legacy of poverty came to an end in Teresa's mind.]

With the addition of a new generation to the family, the novel raises the question whether the cycle of silence and servitude will be reproduced in Teresa's daughter Mia. For the villagers, Mia is merely "une fille de plus" (Saad 45) [one more girl], like her mother: "Fille d'une illettrée, bien entendu. La vie qui l'attend sera peut-être semblable à celle de sa mère" (Saad 45). [The daughter of an illiterate woman, of course. The life that awaits her will perhaps resemble her mother's.] In an attempt to ensure the pattern will not be replicated, Teresa adopts "Madame" rather than her own mother as her model for bringing up her daughter, thus creating a marked contrast between Mia's childhood and her own, and eliminating the resentment that characterized the first generation of mother-daughter relations.[11] Whereas Teresa is illiterate, Mia is educated at a convent, knows how to behave in polite society, and, above all, earns respect --- "depuis toute petite, sa mère lui répète: --- 'Pauvreté n'est pas vice ma fille. Fais-toi respecter!' Et elle se faisait respecter" (Saad 64) [ever since she was very young, her mother kept telling her: --- 'Poverty isn't a vice, my daughter. Earn people's respect!' And she earned their respect]. Despite her mother's precautions, however, Mia is unable to escape the authority and violence of men. When she announces her choice of the church rather than motherhood for her future, her father forces her to postpone her decision, and the rape which occurs after she returns home makes her a mother after all --- an unwilling "reproducer" --- and results in her early death. The rapist, an old friend of her father who has come to the village to promote the cause of Mussolini and "chercher les fils pour la guerre" (Saad 56) [to take their sons away for war] embodies three forms of violence --- rape, fascism, and war --- and serves to create a parallel between war and the violent subjection of women.

Maresa, "l'enfant de la violence" (Saad 57, 78) [the child of violence], represents the hope of permanently breaking the cycle in the fourth generation. Teresa, who finds herself in the role of mother for the second time, "voulait qu'en Maresa se réalisent les . . . rêves de toutes les générations de femmes de sa lignée qui avaient osé espérer autre chose" (Saad 79) [wanted Maresa to achieve the dreams of all the generations of women in her family who had dared to hope for something better]. Achieving this goal involves removing Maresa from the village where men are associated with ignorance, violence, and humiliation. With a decision that recalls her own father's decision to send her to New York, Teresa agrees to allow Maresa to emigrate to Quebec. Contrary to the situation described by Rich, in which the daughter liberates herself by severing her ties with her mother, Teresa cuts the bonds that tie Maresa to her and to the village in order to ensure her future as a free woman --- "Entre elle et la petite, trop de liens créés, trop de fidélité" (Saad 84). [Between her and the little one, too many ties, too much loyalty.] Teresa's suicide after Maresa's departure, "un geste d'amour et de liberté" (Saad 84) [an act of love and freedom], guarantees Maresa will have no reason to return to the village and will complete the voyage of liberation begun with the first emigration: "Une d'entre elles, une de la lignée arriverait enfin en Amérique. Comme une gagnante" (Saad 83). [One of them, someone from her family, would finally make it to America. Victorious.] By the end of the novel, then, Maresa's journey has become a metaphor for freedom from the constraints that led Teresa to return to Italy: "La petite sera seule, elle le sait, et assez forte pour se faire une vie toute neuve sans aucun fantôme pour la harceler" (Saad 85). [The little one will be alone, she is aware of that, but she will be strong enough to forge a new life for herself and will have no ghosts to harry her.] The female proprietor of the old family House has thus prepared a new generation to take charge of its own destiny: unlike Teresa, Maresa possesses the qualities she needs to succeed, and she leaves for Quebec with the negative ties to her past severed, but with a strong, emotional bond to her grandmother, the symbol of the past generations of women who have made her own future possible.

Like *Vers l'Amérique*, Bianca Zagolin's *Une Femme à la fenêtre* [A Woman at the Window] explores mother-daughter relations through the prism of emigration. The novel recounts the life of Aurore, a mother of three who is widowed at age thirty-three and who moves to Quebec from a small Italian town thanks to an invitation from her uncle. Aurore's close relationship with her youngest daughter, who accompanies her on the transatlantic voyage, forms the center of the text, which presents the experiences of two generations facing the New World together.

Aurore's life in Italy is defined by her role as wife and mother, a role handed down over many generations. Traditional rules of behavior, which are associated in the novel with images of repetition, ritual, and immobility, dictate the attitude Aurore should adopt after her husband's death: "elle n'avait qu'à accepter son rôle de femme éplorée et à le jouer jusqu'au bout avec la dignité voilée du sacrifice" (Zagolin 12) [she had only to accept the role of grieving wife and act it out to the full with the veiled dignity of sacrifice]. In reaction to the maternal stoicism expected of her, Aurore senses, but represses the idea, that her life has been diminished by the socially-prescribed constraints of motherhood:

> Après tout, Aurore, ta voie est tracée, tu as tes enfants... Cette phrase suscitait toujours chez elle un malaise qu'elle expliquait mal . . . Par ces quelques mots, on lui refusait un univers qu'elle soupçonnait à peine, auquel elle n'avait jamais eu accès . . . maintenant qu'elle restait seule, on lui en interdisait la possible découverte. Et pourtant, Aurore sentait qu'au delà des confins de sa maternité grouillaient d'innombrables espèces (Zagolin 12).
>
> [After all, Aurore, your path is laid out for you, you have your children... These words always made Aurore feel uneasy, an uneasiness she found it hard to explain . . . With these few words, she was barred from a world whose existence she hardly imagined, which she had never had access to . . . and now she was alone, she was being denied the possibility of ever discovering it. And yet Aurore sensed that beyond the confines of motherhood lay a world teeming with other possibilities.]

With her awakening consciousness of the motherhood-versus-freedom question, she experiences the same silent alienation as does Teresa in *Vers l'Amérique*, and her feeling of emptiness is reflected in the activity of waiting and in the recurrent images of cold, whiteness and suffocation used to characterize her life --- "sa vie consistait à attendre, sans jamais se lasser . . . Attendre était sa façon d'exister" (Zagolin 17) [her life consisted of waiting, without ever becoming weary. Waiting was her way of existing]. Meanwhile, the marks left on her body by household chores are the physical signs of a daily routine that produces psychological scars, a corporeal inscription of her role as mother which negates her identity as a woman and sexual being: "son corps arborait les marques d'un quotidien banal et pourtant plein de périls: rougeurs, écorchures, brûlures, cicatrices" (Zagolin 15) [her body bore the marks of a daily routine that was banal and yet full of danger: red patches, scratches, burns, scars].

In Aurore's relationship with her daughter during this period, the traditional mother-daughter roles are reversed, and Adalie assumes the role of protector. The antithesis of her mother, Adalie is associated with freshness and life, and provides a counterweight to the images of cold and death used to describe her mother: "sa mère lui était reconnaissante d'être là, comme un lien charnel avec la vie. . . . la tendre et pétillante enfant finirait bien par rentrer de l'école, fidèle comme une aube, et Aurore serait sauvée, une fois de plus" (Zagolin 10) [her mother was grateful for her being there, for providing a real link with life. . . . the affectionate, sparkling child would finally come home as always, as faithful as the dawn, and Aurore would be saved once again]. In spite of her mother's name, it is Adalie, not Aurore, who represents the light and warmth necessary for growth and development.

Moving to Quebec represents a second birth for Aurore and further strengthens her relationship with her daughter. Mother and daughter work together to plan their shared future, and their preparations for departure "cimentèrent leur complicité de femmes" (Zagolin 37) [cemented their complicity as women]. In Quebec, the pattern of reversal in their relationship continues as Adalie takes on the role of teacher. In particular, she instructs her mother in French and in the history of Canada, thereby providing her with the means to establish roots in Quebec: "mot par mot, page par page, elle lui apportait le pays; une fois de plus c'est elle qui enracinait Aurore dans la vie. L'enfant avait toujours pressenti que cette tâche lui revenait et elle l'accomplissait le plus naturellement du monde" (Zagolin 59) [one word at a time, one page at a time, she brought the country to her mother; once again it was she who provided Aurore with roots in life. The child had always sensed that this was her task and she carried it out most naturally]. For Aurore, who now identifies with the early settlers of Quebec, language is synonymous with life, and learning French is equated with the exploration and conquest of a virgin land, "un territoire jusque-là inexploré" (Zagolin 59) [a formerly unexplored territory].[12] The new world she appropriates through the lessons given by Adalie fills the void in her life and stands in contrast to the life refused her in Italy.

The second stage of Aurore's awakening leads to her rebirth as a woman with sexual desires. Irigaray's analysis of desire in relation to the mother --- "le désir d'elle, son désir à elle (Irigarary 1981, 15)[13] [desire of her, her own desire] --- emphasizes its repression in patriarchal societies, and she stresses the importance of freeing mothers from their one-dimensional maternal role, insisting that they should not have to give up being women in order to be mothers. In *Une Femme à la fenêtre*, Adalie, along with Aurore's lover Sebastien, enables Aurore to move beyond her maternal function, "cette nichée où elle avait coulé son être" (Zagolin 76) [that nest she had poured her whole being into], and to reintegrate desire into her life, "son désir qu'elle regardait hardiment en face" (Zagolin 76) [her desire she boldly looked in the face]. The transformation of the old Aurore, "celle qui avait vécu là-bas, selon les règles des autres, vide comme une poupée de porcelaine" (Zagolin 71) [the old Aurore, the one who in Italy had lived by the rules of other, as empty as a porcelain doll], into the woman who expresses her passion in Sebastien's forest home is highlighted in a series of mythical and religious images. In particular, the allusions to "Sleeping Beauty" and the life of Christ convey the notion of re-awakening and resurrection, and emphasize the new role of Aurore's body as the locus of her desire: "Aurore s'était faite chair et était descendue sur terre pour réintégrer sa demeure et ses droits" (Zagolin 91). [Aurore had been made flesh and had come into the world to reclaim her home and her rights.] Whereas Aurore's uncle, who replaced her husband as the representative of paternal authority, would have condemned her metamorphosis --- "aurait frappé Aurore d'un jugement sans appel" (Zagolin 72) [would have handed down a verdict without appeal] --- Adalie understands and encourages her mother's liaison with Sebastien: "la petite, elle, comprendrait, comprenait déjà" (Zagolin 73) [the little one would understand, already understood.] Finally able to reconcile her roles as woman and mother,[14] Aurore moves from the position of "la délaissée sur cette terre" [abandoned woman] to that of "Aurore la conquérante" (Zagolin 78) [Aurore the conqueror], a re-birth that recalls Maresa's destiny as "une gagnante" (Saad 83) [a winner] in *Vers l'Amérique*, and that is reflected in the name "Aurore" (Zagolin 80).[15]

Teresa's awakening as a woman is accompanied by a rebellion

against the patriarchal order and the expression of feelings she sensed but could not formulate in Italy: "le passé lui devient de plus en plus intolérable. Toutes ces années d'acceptation, ravalées dans un sourire, lui montaient à la gorge comme un poison. . . . Avec la passion de vivre, s'étaient réveillées la rancoeur et la haine, et l'amour lui dévoilait le ressentiment" (Zagolin 88-9) [she found it increasingly difficult to stand the past. All those years of acceptance, swallowed with a smile, now welled up in her throat like a poison. . . . Her passion for life had also awakened bitterness and hatred, and love uncovered resentment]. Unlike the illiterate Teresa, who was unable to express her revolt, Aurore possesses the language to convey hers --- "des mots qu'elle avait tus pendant toute une vie, alors qu'elle aurait dû les crier à tue-tête, pour se sauver. Des milliers et des milliers de mots" (Zagolin 90) [words she had kept quiet her whole life when she should have shouted them out at the top of her voice. Thousands and thousands of words]. These words express her new feminist consciousness, her "fureur de femme" [her woman's anger] (Zagolin 90), and she uses them to contest the silencing and disempowerment of women:

> Haine sourde pour les hommes, surtout, des millions d'hommes sans visage qui, dans tous les pays du monde, faisaient la loi et réglaient tout entre eux . . . Des foules d'hommes omniprésents et pourtant toujours absents des lieux essentiels. Son père, son mari, son frère. Les hommes lui avient offert leur bras pour qu'elle s'y appuie . . . En échange, elle avait renoncé à sa force et à sa voix (Zagolin 90).
>
> [A gnawing hatred of men, above all, of the millions of faceless men who, in every country of the world, make the rules and settle everything among themselves . . . Throngs of men everywhere and yet who are always absent from the most important places. Her father, her husband, her brother. The men who had offered her their arms so she could lean on them . . . in exchange, she had given up her strength and her voice.]

Aurore's new-found voice and strength lead to her reinstatement in the role of teacher. In her desire to improve the position of women, she promises to pass on to her daughter the lessons she herself has learned: "elle devait lui apprendre l'essentiel pour qu'elle pût se forger une âme à sa guise. Cela, elle se l'était juré et cette promesse avait approfondi leur connivence" (Zagolin 93) [she must teach her the most important lessons so she would be able to forge an identity of her own. Aurore had vowed to do this, and that promise strengthened their complicity]. At this climactic point in the novel, the affection and complicity between mother and daughter are presented as their joint triumph. The symbolic "couronne de laurier" (Zagolin 103) [laurel wreath] Adalie is awarded at school represents her mother's victory too, and the second section of the text ends with images of harmony, plenitude, and well-being: "Jamais elles ne s'étaient senties plus près l'une de l'autre . . . Aurore et son enfant habitait enfin la même terre et leur enracinement s'achevait par les forces alliées de l'amour et de la parole. . . Leur corps se balançait à l'unisson sur un pas cadencé" (Zagolin 104). [Never had they felt so close. . . Aurore and her child finally inhabited the same country, and the power of love and language together had enabled them to put down roots. Their body moved harmoniously as they walked in step with each other.] Here, the references to unity, shared territory, and a common body suggest that their relationship based on reciprocity has enabled both mother and daughter to move forward together and to appropriate a new territory.

Sébastien's death and Aurore's descent into madness in the final part of the novel lead to a further reversal and threaten the mother-daughter harmony "qui, jusque'là, semblait sans déchirure" (Zagolin 180) [which had seemed unbroken until this point]. Despair now replaces plenitude as Aurore, prey to nightmares and hallucinations, is unable to resign herself to the role of "épouse éplorée" [grieving wife] she assumed after the death of her husband. In this situation, Adalie again becomes the protector --- "Adalie, Adalie, sauve-moi, Adalie, sauve-moi" (Zagolin 125) [save me, Adalie, save me]; while Adalie assumes the role of mother and nourisher, Aurore adopts that of child: "les rôles sont inversés. C'est Adalie qui la gronde comme une enfant; elle la dorlote aussi, la console, lui dit quand se lever, ce qu'elle doit manger" (Zagolin 185) [their roles are reversed. It is Adalie who scolds her like a child; she pampers her too, and consoles her, tells her when to get up, what she should eat]. On this occasion, however, caring for a mother she has difficulty recognizing proves difficult, and Adalie's rebellion against the maternal role recalls her mother's own revolt against the limitations of motherhood:

> Adalie regarde, muette et impuissante. Parfois, elle suffoque de rage contre ce fardeau trop lourd pour elle, si jeune . . . Elle voudrait secouer Aurore dans son lit, hurler qu'elle n'en peut plus, qu'elle veut danser à la corde avec ses amies . . . Et qu'on enlève cette morte couchée là-haut qui n'est pas vraiment sa mère (Zagolin 175).
>
> [Adalie looks on, silent and powerless. Sometimes, she chokes with

> anger at this burden which is too heavy for her, she who is so young ... She would like to shake Aurore in her bed, to scream that she can't take any more, that she wants to go skipping with her friends . . . And would someone please take away that dead woman lying upstairs who isn't really her mother.]

The division between mother and daughter is not long-lived, however, since Adalie realizes her mother's identity and her own are interconnected, and she does not wish to sever the ties between them. As in *Vers l'Amérique*, it is Aurore's suicide, like Teresa's, that frees the daughter to pursue her future: "Une nouvelle héroïne surgira pour prendre la relève et cette héroïne, ce sera Adalie" (Zagolin 189). [A new heroine will rise up to take her place and that heroine will be Adalie.] Like the end of *Vers l'Amérique*, the epilogue of *Une Femme à la fenêtre* contains images of beauty, warmth, and plenitude as Adalie, symbolically positioned "au sommet" [at the summit] prepares to forge her life in Quebec (Zagolin 201). Aurore's legacy to her daughter is thus not one of resignation and capitulation, like the heritage she herself had received, but one of self-realization. In this sense, Adalie "croit à la beauté du monde, elle croit à la vie qu'Aurore lui a léguée" (Zagolin 201) [believes in the beauty of the world, believes in the life Aurore has bequeathed her].

While the mother-daughter relationship in *Une Femme à la fenêtre* is characterized by mutual support, the emotion at the center of Ying Chen's third novel is, as the title suggests, *L'Ingratitude* [Ingratitude]. Narrated by the daughter Yan-zi, whose mother labels her a "fille ingrate" (Chen 10, 24, 41, 64) [an ungrateful daughter], the novel recounts the daughter's struggle for independence and her decision to commit suicide as a way of separating herself from her mother. The narrative alternates between past and present, life and death, juxtaposing passages in which Yan-zi looks back on her life with those in which, "flottant au dessus de cette fumée d'encens" (Chen 16) [floating above the incense smoke], she hovers over her family and friends at her funeral. Unlike the end of *Vers l'Amérique*, where Teresa's death ensures Maresa will have "aucun fantôme pour la harceler" (Saad 85) [no ghosts to harry her], the beginning of *L'Ingratitude* announces Yan-zi's intention to haunt her mother in order to give her a guilty conscience --- "je brûle d'envie de voir maman souffrir à la vue de mon cadavre. Souffrir jusqu'à vomir son sang" (Chen 18). [I'm dying to see Mama suffer at the sight of my dead body. Suffer so much she throws up blood.] Yan-zi presents herself as an unwanted daughter who is tired of trying to please a tyrannical mother, and her picture of their relationship, which is full of black humor, powerfully conveys the link between her suicidal tendencies and her matricidal feelings: "J'étais prête à m'empoisonner ou à étrangler cette femme" (Chen 84) [I was ready to poison myself or strangle that woman].

Yan-zi portrays her mother as a classic case of a woman limited to "la pure et simple fonction maternelle" [the pure and simple maternal function]: her role as mother defines her entire identity and reduces her daughter to the corresponding "fonction d'enfant" (Irigaray 1981, 66) [function of child]. Consequently, the mother describes herself exclusively in terms of "son expérience de mère" (Chen 12) [her experience as mother], while recurrent references to imprisonment underscore the daughter's entrapment in the role of child: "je suis à jamais son enfant à elle" (Chen 13), "j'avais vécu en tant que l'enfant de ma mère. Il me fallait mourir autrement" (Chen 24). [I am forever her child. . . I had lived as my mother's child. I had to die differently.] The question at the center of the novel is thus the same as one raised by Irigaray: "comment pour nous, les filles, avoir un rapport personnel et se constituer une identité par rapport à quelqu'une qui n'est qu'une fonction?" (Irigaray 1981, 86) [how can we daughters have a personal relationship with and create an identity in relation to someone who is only a function?]

Images related to food and the body convey both the mother's desire for fusion with her daughter and the daughter's feeling of suffocation. A short dialogue illustrates the mother's attempts to maintain Yan-zi in the role of daughter:

> - J'ai envie d'être moi, maman.
> - Tu ne peux pas être toi sans être ma fille.
> - Je suis d'abord moi.
> - Tu as vécu d'abord dans mon ventre (Chen 116).
>
> [- I want to be myself, Mama.
> - You can't be yourself without being my daughter.
> - I want to be me first.
> - You first lived in my womb.]

A symbol of origins and motherhood, the womb represents the original fusion of mother and daughter that the mother wishes to perpetuate: "elle prenait ma main et la plaçait sur le côté droit de son ventre et me disait: Tu es là. Elle formulait cette phrase au présent, comme si je n'avais pas encore quitté son corps. Comment puis-je cesser de me soucier de toi? ajoutait-elle, tu es un morceau de ma chair" (Chen 96) [she used to take my hand and place it on the right side of her stomach and would say: You are there. She formulated this sentence in the present as if I had not yet left her body. How can I stop worrying about you? she would add, you are a piece of my flesh]. The use of the present tense denies the possibility of putting an end to the fusion and leaves no room for the daughter to develop a separate identity. Other passages relate fusion and reproduction through the mother's desire to replicate herself in her daughter: "Je ne devrais vivre qu'à travers elle. Elle cherchait à s'incarner en moi . . . J'étais censée devenir la reproduction la plus exacte possible de ma mère. J'étais sa fille" (Chen 97). [She thought I should live only through her. She was trying to take over my body. . . . I was supposed to become the most faithful replica of my mother possible. I was her daughter.] Further corporeal images suggest that in order to fashion her daughter in her own image, the mother inhabits her body, thus creating a reverse form of pregnancy in which the daughter now carries her unwanted mother: "vous qui vivez partiellement dans mon corps sans que je vous aie invitée" (Chen 23) [you who live partly in my body without my having invited you to]. For Yan-zi, then, the womb is equated with non-separation, and repudiation of the womb symbolizes rejection of the mother: "J'étais donc sortie de là. De ce ventre mou, sale et gonflé de gras. J'aurais préféré naître d'une pierre ou d'une plante sans nom" (Chen 20). [So I had come out of there. Out of that flabby, dirty stomach, rolling in fat. I would rather have been born from a stone or an unnamed plant.] In similar fashion, the scar from the caesarian on her mother's stomach stands as a permanent reminder of Yan-zi's lack of freedom and of her mother's possessiveness: "la ligne foncée sur ce ventre étranger me criait en pleine figure: Tu ne peux pas m'échapper, c'est moi qui t'ai formée, ton corps et ton esprit, avec ma chair et mon sang --- tu es à moi, entièrement à moi" (Chen 20) [the dark line on that foreign stomach screamed at me: You can't escape me, I'm the one who formed you with my own flesh and blood --- formed your body and your mind --- you belong to me, to me alone].

Irigaray observes that in a patriarchal society the womb is often perceived not as a place of nourishment but as a devouring mouth --- "la matrice, non pensée comme lieu du premier séjour où l'on devient corps, est fantasmée comme bouche dévorante" (Irigarary 1981, 24) [the womb, no longer conceptualized as one's first home, where one becomes a body, is fantasized as a devouring mouth]. In *L'Ingratitude*, images related to food and eating reinforce the daughter's negative vision of a devouring mother-womb who denies her the right to exist: "J'avais parfois l'impression qu'elle avait envie de m'avaler vivante" (Chen 121).

[I sometimes had the impression she wanted to swallow me alive.] Other characters associated with the mother's rule use similar images. Chun, the mother's ally and her potential successor in Yan-zi's life, expresses his love in similar cannibalistic terms --- "je t'aime tant que j'ai envie de t'avaler tout rond" (Chen 96) [I love you so much I want to swallow you whole] --- and Yan-zi's feeling of being devoured continues even after death as she haunts the cremation banquet: "J'ai soudain la stupide impression d'être mangée par les invités de maman" (Chen 63) [I suddenly have the stupid feeling I'm being eaten by Mama's guests]. These recurrent references to being swallowed convey the destructive effects of the suffocating maternal desire for fusion and its negative impact on the mother-daughter relationship.

Irigaray's discussion of mother-daughter relations also emphasizes the importance of communication ("parler") as a form of nourishment: "il est important aussi de parler en nourrissant un enfant pour qu'il ne vive pas ce nourrissage comme un gavage violent, comme viol" (Irigaray 1981, 29) [it is also important to talk while feeding a child so that he will not experience this nourishment as violent force-feeding, as a violation]. The relationship between Yan-zi and her mother is characterized by lack of communication, and the mother's refrain, "je fais ça pour ton bien" (Chen 21) [I'm doing it for your own good], serves to justify all her decisions regarding her daughter. Yan-zi explicitly refers to her mother's behavior as a "viol" [rape] --- "vouloir s'occuper du bien des autres n'était-il pas une tentative de pillage et de viol?" (Chen 21) [isn't wanting to take charge of the 'good' of others an attempted rape and form of looting?] --- and she experiences her mother's care as a form of "gavage" [force-feeding] rather than nurturance. Food and eating thus become symbols not of the mother-as-nurturer but of the mother-as-force-feeder. In her role as daughter, Yan-zi is required to dine with her mother every day, is expected never to leave a piece of food in her plate, and, by extension, to "digest" all her mother's ideas --- "Elle n'hésitait pas à me dévoiler toutes ses vérités à elle que je devais, à son avis, digérer sans difficulté puisque j'étais sa fille" (Chen 52) [she didn't hesitate to reveal all *her* truths to me, truths she thought I should have no problem digesting since I was her daughter]. In this sense, Yan-zi's relationship with her mother is reduced to one of eating --- "consommer/être consommées" (Irigaray 1979, 11) [eating/being eaten] --- and, like Irigaray, she calls for an end to the excessive feeding: "Tu m'apportes à manger. Tu me/te donnes à manger. Mais tu me/te donnes trop comme si tu voulais me remplir toute entière . . . Tu te mets dans ma bouche et j'étouffe. Mets-toi moins en moi" (Irigaray 1979, 9). [You bring me food. You give me/you to eat. But you give me/you too much as if you want to fill me up completely . . . You put yourself in my mouth and I am suffocating. Put less of you in me.]

For Yan-zi, severing all ties with her mother appears to be the only means of attaining selfhood, and suicide is the form of "radical surgery" (Rich 236) she envisages: "Il fallait donc détruire cette reproduction à tout prix. Il fallait tuer sa fille" (Chen 97) [That resemblance had to be destroyed at any cost. Her daughter had to be killed.] The "séparation brutale" (Chen 12) takes place in several stages. As a first step, Yan-zi offers her virginity to a man she hardly knows, thus making herself unmarriageable, an act of defiance intended to anger her mother --- "je m'étais fait déchirer le corps. Maman avait donc pondu un corps qui ne valait plus rien. . . . en me livrant aux bras d'un inconnu, je n'avais pensé qu'à elle" (Chen 80, 87). [I had got myself torn open. So Mama had produced a body that wasn't worth anything anymore. . . . as I abandoned myself to the arms of an unknown man, I had thought only of her.] Leaving the maternal home-womb and spending the night in the transitory space of the railway station constitutes the second stage of the separation, and composing the suicide note, designed to make the mother "démissionner de son poste de mère" (Chen 13) [resign from her position of mother], signals the preparation of the final stage, the liberation through death that is to give Yan-zi her individuality: "quand je ne serai plus rien, je serai moi" (Chen 24) [when I am no longer anything, I will be me].[16]

While many episodes emphasize Yan-zi's suicidal fanasies, other passages problematize her apparent matrophobia, and suggest the existence of more positive feelings towards her mother. Irigaray argues that if mother-daughter relations are to improve, "le premier geste, c'est de se réconcilier avec la mère en soi parce qu'on la introjectée, notre mère, donc il faut essayer de faire la paix avec cette mère-là. . . . faire la paix avec sa mère réelle est aussi important" (Irigaray 1981, 62) [the first step is to become reconciled with the mother in ourselves, because our mother has been interjected into us --- so we must try to make peace with that mother. . . . making peace with one's real mother is important too]. Although the most violent images in *L'Ingratitude* convey Yan-zi's desire to expel the "interjected" mother "qui vi[t] partiellement dans mon corps" (Chen 23) [who lives partly in my body], the end of the novel suggests a certain reconciliation with the mother. First, Yan-zi recognizes the need to come to terms with the mother in herself: "On ne peut pas se détourner de sa mère sans se débarrasser de soi-même" (Chen

129). [You can't reject your mother without losing yourself at the same time.] At the same time, her mother appears less authoritarian and more of a victim herself: "je découvre pour la première fois que maman est en fait aussi innocente et vulnérable comme les autres . . . moins solide. Je l'aime mieux ainsi. J'aurais voulu le lui dire. Mais c'est trop tard" (Chen 131). [I'm discovering for the first time that Mama is in fact as innocent and as vulnerable as the others . . . less solid. I like her better that way. I would have liked to tell her so. But it's too late.] The positive image of nourishing maternal milk now replaces that of force-feeding as Yan-zi recognizes a mother may have worthwhile advice to give her daughter: "il était peut-être tout naturel que j'aie besoin de conseils et que maman ait des conseils à donner. Une mère devait avoir le lait dont sa fille avait besoin. Je me félicitais d'avoir trouvé cette comparaison et j'étais sûre que maman aimerait l'entendre" (Chen 121) [it was perhaps only natural that I need advice and that Mama have advice to give. A mother should have the milk her daughter needs. I was very pleased to have come up with that comparison and I was sure mama would like to hear it]. Furthermore, although Yan-zi at first declares her mother "son ennemi" (Chen 90) [her enemy], she later recognizes her father's role in creating the conflictual mother-daughter relationship. His neglect of his wife makes the daughter solely responsible for making her mother happy, a task she can never accomplish alone. In this sense, "c'était lui qui m'avait créé, en quelque sorte, une ennemie" (Chen 30) [in a sense, it was he who had made an enemy for me],[17] and Yan-zi at this point acknowledges the injustice on her part of directing her anger at her mother alone: "Il n'était pas juste de me venger de maman seulement. Mais que pouvais-je faire? Papa était intellectuel, donc imperméable. Mon suicide l'intéresserait moins que l'assassinat d'un président américain. On ne frappait que ceux qui pouvait être frappés" (Chen 30). [It wasn't fair to take it all out on Mama. But what could I do? Papa was an intellectual and therefore untouchable. My suicide would interest him less than the assassination of an American president. You only hit those who can be hit.] Through Yan-zi's realization of her father's destructive role, Chen reveals how the treatment of mothers in a patriarchal society harms their relationship with their daughters. Neglected as a woman by her husband, Yan-zi's mother devotes all her time to mothering, thereby preventing her daughter's self-realization, while the real "enemy," the father, remains untouched and apparently untouchable --- "imperméable" (Chen 30).

By the end of the novel, Yan-zi understands the nature of "the loss of the daughter to the mother, the mother to the daughter" (Rich

237). In the final pages, she acknowledges the tragedy and regrets the loss: "jamais on ne devrait trahir sa mère" (Chen 122) [one should never betray one's mother].[18] As she re-reads what was to be a hypocritical suicide note that falsely declared her love for her mother --- complete with fake tears --- the declaration and the tears become sincere: "cette lettre mensongère, cette fausse déclaration d'amour à maman me semblent maintenant devenue une chose sincère. Je voulais la frapper très fort . . . mais j'en souffrais avant elle" (Chen 122) [that deceitful letter, that false declaration of love to my mother now seem to have become sincere. I wanted to hit her very hard . . . but now I was suffering before her]. The novel thus closes with an affirmation of the value of the mother-daughter bond, a reversal in which the daughter recognizes her own "ingratitude," and the final image, at once a symbol of memory and of re-birth, makes "maman" the last word of the text. This final cry carries with it the daughter's hope for a new model of mother-daughter relations in the future: "à travers le brouillard de cette mémoire, me parvient, comme une lamentation enchantée, une dernière voix humaine, le cri d'un nourrison peut-être:/Maman!" (Chen 133). [through the mists of memory, like an enchanted lament, there comes a last human voice, the cry of a baby maybe:/Mama!]

Les Jardins de cristal, [The Crystal Gardens] Nadia Ghalem's first novel, is an example of "psychiatric fiction" (Yalom 13), an account of mental breakdown and the accompanying search for sanity, rebirth, and identity.[19] The text, which takes the form of a letter and a manuscript sent by a daughter to her mother, announces from the outset the daughter's desire for reconciliation. This desire has prompted her to explore in writing the role played in her mental disorder by the Algerian War and her relationship with her parents, particularly her mother.

During the narrator's childhood in Algeria, the mother-daughter relationship is characterized by opposition, distance, and mutual incomprehension. Like the narrator of *L'Ingratitude*, the daughter (Chafia) feels unwanted and expresses her resentment of her mother: "Mère, tu as eu tort de me haïr. . . . Mère tu as eu tort de me punir" (Ghalem 13). [Mother, you were wrong to hate me. . . . Mother you were wrong to punish me.] The first image is thus that of the Terrible Mother --- authoritarian, cold, and uncaring --- "une femme terrible que l'amour maternel rendait autoriataire, une mère qui ne s'imaginait pas que l'on pût exister en dehors d'elle" (Ghalem 7) [a dreadful woman whose maternal love had made her authoritarian, a mother who could not imagine one could exist independently of her]. At this point, mother and daughter are described in terms of their differences: whereas the daughter's response to her situation involves anger, flight, and madness, the mother's is characterized by faith, silence, and action --- conflicting attitudes symbolized by "ta foi et ma folie" (Ghalem 26) [your faith and my madness]. Above all, Chafia rejects the image of motherhood as enslavement, equating the role of mother with that of domestic animal: "Vos cris, vos histoires de vaisselle-cuisine-bébé-fatigue. Vos cris qui nous blessent les oreilles, parce que vous n'avez jamais eu le loisir de rêvasser. Vous faites partie des animaux domestiques de l'Homme, de mon père" (Ghalem 24). [Your cries, your dishes-cooking-baby-exhaustion stories. Your cries that hurt our ears because you've never had time to daydream. You are one of Man's --- of my father's --- domestic animals.] In particular, she is unable to understand her mother's resignation and unwillingness to rebel against her role: "je pense à toi, ma mère, et j'essaie de comprendre pourquoi tu ne t'es jamais révoltée" (Ghalem 59) [I think of you, my mother, and I try to understand why you never rebelled].

Like Yan-zi, the young Chafia fears she will become a replica of her mother, an embodiment of the same "féminité-victime" (Ghalem 21) [femininity-victim]. She expresses her matrophobia on several occasions, repeatedly associating motherhood with meaninglessness: "j'ai été effrayée de te retrouver en moi" (Ghalem 7); "J'espérais ne pas vous ressembler" (Ghalem 24); "mon problème, c'est de continuer cette vie qui ressemble au destin de ma mère. Je ne voulais pas, je ne voulais pas du tout cela, une vie de femme sans rime ni raison" (Ghalem 38). [Discovering you in me has been frightening; I hoped I wouldn't be like you; my problem is how to continue this life which resembles my mother's fate. I didn't want that, I absolutely didn't want it --- a meaningless woman's life.] Fear of reproducing the mother leads to the desire to break the chain of suffering that links and imprisons generations of mothers and daughters: "mais à pleurer de mère en fille, nous risquons de faire une chaîne de larmes qui nous retiendra prisonnières de la même eau empoisonnée et qui risque de nous noyer" (Ghalem 26). [But through weeping from mother to daughter we may create a chain of tears that will hold us prisoner in the same poisoned water and may drown us.] A short dialogue similar to the one in *L'Ingratitude* encapsulates the mother-daughter, resignation-revolt, paradigm:

> Et tes idées a toi, maman?
> Je suis une femme. Ma maison est propre. Mes enfants sont élevés.
> Et ton existence à toi?
> C'est le destin.

Tu es sans révolte?
Je suis entre les mains de Dieu (Ghalem 19).

[And your ideas, Mama?
I'm a woman. My house is clean. I've raised my children.
And *your* life?
It's fate.
Don't you feel any revolt?
I'm in God's hands.]

Viewing the pairs in the paradigm as mutually exclusive, Chafia rejects her mother and opts for the side that represents "LA LIBERTE" (Ghalem 20) [FREEDOM].

The divisions between mother and daughter are reinforced by references to the Algerian War, which took place during Chafia's childhood. The collective struggle for independence mirrors the individual fight for freedom and is described through similar images of physical and psychological suffering. Recurrent references to violence and death convey the horror of growing up during the war: "Chers parents . . . Regardez, le corps de la petite fille polie n'est plus que pulsation. Il crache à flots le sang de la guerre et le bouillonnement vermeil de sa jeune existence broyée dedans. Regardez le flot gelé de souffrance intolérée, inacceptée" (Ghalem 13). [Dear parents . . . look, the body of your polite little girl is nothing but a pulse. It's spewing out torrents of blood from the war and the bright red froth of her young life ground up in it. Look at the frozen waves of intolerable, unaccepted suffering.] A second series of images evokes Chafia's withdrawal into herself in an attempt to escape the war outside. Recurrent metaphors involving cold, hard surfaces describe her isolation and alienation --- "moi, je devenais marbre, je refroidissais à la surface" (Ghalem 14) [I was turning into marble, I was becoming cold on the surface] --- while references to glass containers suggest her separation from the exterior world: "Alors je me suis sauvée, je me suis retirée en moi-même, dans cette cage de verre" (Ghalem 12). [So I ran away, I retreated into myself, into this glass cage.] The appearance of this interior world, alternately called "boule de verre" (Ghalem 20) [glass ball], "cage de verre" (Ghalem 12) [glass cage], and "cloche de verre" (Ghalem 49) [glass bell jar], is reminiscent of Sylvia Plath's "bell jar" and signals Chafia's flight into insanity. Subsequently, the same images of bombs, explosions, and destruction describe both the Algerian War and Chafia's internal fight against madness: "je suis prisonnière d'une chimie qui me fait une guerre intérieure. Le danger ne viendra pas du dehors. Il m'habite. Je suis minée et personne ne peut me désamorcer. Je vais sauter comme une bombe" (Ghalem 39). [I am the prisoner of chemicals that are waging a war within me. The danger won't come from outside. It lives inside me. I'm mined and no one can defuse me. I'm going to blow up like a bomb.]

Chafia's insanity is at once an escape from war and a refuge from the socially-prescribed role of woman-as-mother. As such, it constitutes a form of "liberation" that foregrounds the gender-related aspects of women's mental disorders while stressing the effects mothers have on their daughters' mental health. In this sense, insanity is Chafia's means of defense against the pressure to conform:

> la folie, sans être une excuse, peut devenir mon alliée. Elle est ma protection contre moi-même est les autres. C'est un passeport aussi, tres spécial. . . . Il faut donc que je sois folle aux yeux des autres pour pouvoir enfin devenir tout à fait moi-même et cette étrange libération agit comme une guérison temporaire (Ghalem 106).
>
> [madness --- without being an excuse --- can become my ally. It's my protection against myself and others. It's a passport too, of a very special kind. . . . I have to be mad in the eyes of others in order to finally become completely myself, and this strange form of liberation acts as a temporary cure.]

Her madness is thus both a form of protest against and a protection from patriarchal society and its imprisonment of women in traditional roles. For this reason, Chafia is able to affirm, "derrière ma folie, je suis parfaitement socialisée et normalisée. Cependant, je l'ai été si parfaitement, que la vie était devenue pire que la mort" (Ghalem 38) [behind my madness, I am perfectly socialized and normal. But I've been socialized so well that life had become worse than death].

In her revolt, Chafia aligns herself with poets and children, and against soldiers, politicians, and psychiatrists.[20] The latter, the men she holds responsible for producing her illness and determining its treatment, are associated with metal, glass, and destruction: "Je les hais. Je les hais de l'orient à l'occident et du sud au nord avec leur médecine et leur politique et tout ce qu'ils ont fabriqué de verre et de métal" (Ghalem 40) [I hate them. I hate them from east to west and from north to south, with their medicine and their politics and everything they've made from glass and metal]. Chafia's account of her treatment at the hands of inimical male doctors emphasizes the tyranny of her so-called healers and makes it clear that the same patriarchal attitudes that defined limiting female roles are now reflected in the institutions treating women for failing to conform to those roles.[21] As representatives of patriarchal law and order, these "superviseurs de la folie" (Ghalem 70) [supervisors of madness] who classify Chafia's illness and attempt to cure her --- usually by prescribing drugs --- merely create another form of imprisonment. The often surreal, hallucinatory images that reveal Chafia's mental state repeatedly portray her as "une grenouille au milieu d'un jardin de cristal" (Ghalem 122) [a frog in a crystal garden].[22] The crystal garden, the domain of doctors and soldiers, represents a male-dominated world whose metal and glass shards mutilate the bodies of those who seek to escape it. For Chafia, the imposition of dehumanizing labels --- the tentative diagnosis is schizophrenia --- in an attempt to categorize and contain her symptoms reflects the uncaring attitudes of the inhumane world she rejects: "vous avez beau me codifier dans vos fiches perforées, me décoder dans vos cartes numérotées et me harceler de vos mots mécaniques, je resterai, en tant que femme et pour toujours, le crapaud au sein du diamant coupant de votre humanité minéralisée" (Ghalem 72). [You can try all you want to encode me in your punch cards, to decode me on your index cards, to harass me with your mechanical words: as a woman I will forever be the toad at the heart of the sharp-edged diamond of your mineralized humanity.]

Unlike her mother, then, Chafia chooses rebellion and self-determination rather than resignation and conformity --- "j'ai sauté la clôture" (Ghalem 59) [I jumped over the fence] --- and her insanity further separates her from her mother, who is unable to understand the role she has played in creating her daughter's mental state: "ma mère, elle, est comme ces gros pays surpuissants qui ouvrent des yeux de vierges offensées devant les cataclysmes qu'ils ont provoqués" (Ghalem 78) [my mother is like the big superpowers that open their eyes wide like offended virgins when faced with the cataclysmic events they themselves have caused]. The reconciliation between mother and daughter occurs, however, after Chafia has become a mother herself. As in *L'Ingratitude*, Chafia is reconciled with both her real mother and the mother in herself.[23] Freed from the earlier image of the Terrible Mother, "celle qui me cachait la femme que tu étais vraiment" (Ghalem 8) [the one who hid the woman you really were], Chafia, like Yan-zi, now sees her mother as victim, and her feelings of resentment give way to compassion and affection.[24] She mirrors Yan-zi too in her desire for a mother who would share more of her feelings --- "je t'aurais sans doute mieux aimée si tu t'étais montrée à moi humaine et fragile" (Ghalem 8)

[I would certainly have liked you better if you had shown yourself to be human and fragile]. "Foi" [faith] and "folie" [madness], the apparently irreconcilable symbols of difference, now become signs of resemblance --- complementary forms of escape and hope: "Pauvre maman, entre ta foi et ma folie, il n'y a qu'une mince paroi transparente. Un souffle. Ce sont pour toi et moi des portes royales qui s'ouvrent sur l'aube qui lavera nos souffrances" (Ghalem 26). [Poor Mama, between your faith and my madness, there is only a thin transparent screen. A breath. For you and me, they are the royal gates opening onto the dawn that will wash away our suffering.] This recognition enables Chafia to focus on what she and her mother have in common as women --- "Je suis sa fille, mais nous sommes toutes les deux des femmes qui ont lutté, aimé, et souffert. Un jour, je l'ai retrouvée comme une soeur, jeune dans sa tête et dans son coeur" (Ghalem 115). [I am her daughter, but we are both women who have struggled, loved, and suffered. One day I found her again, like a sister, still young in her mind and her heart.] At the same time, her mother makes similar adjustments and moves out of a purely maternal role: "tu ne me traitais plus comme ton enfant chétive. Tu admettais mon existence propre" (Ghalem 9) [you no longer treated me as your sickly child. You recognized I had a life of my own]. Subsequently, the images of healing and rebirth associated with daughter's recovery center on the figure of the mother. During their ten-day reunion, the mother is portrayed as giving birth to her daughter for a second time, a birth that heralds a new kind of relationship between the two women --- "c'était comme si tu m'avais donné la vie une seconde fois. Sans t'en rendre compte, tu me fournissais les moyens de briser les murs de la folie" (Ghalem 8) [it was as if you had given birth to me a for second time. Without realizing it, you gave me the means to break the walls of my madness]. Formerly a negative model, the mother has become the daughter's "critère de référence" (Ghalem 136) [point of reference], and the ties that now bind them are those of mutual support. This new-found "rapport de réciprocité de femme à femme" (Irigaray1981, 86) [reciprocal woman-to-woman relationship] foregrounds both the central role of the mother --- as opposed to the male-dominated psychiatric profession --- in restoring her daughter's sanity, and the need for mothers and daughters to recognize each other as women with common fears and desires.

As a path to sanity --- both her own and that of society --- Chafia resolves to promote maternal values, and thus turns her reconciliation with her mother into a strong political statement. As a mother, Chafia becomes a strong proponent of what Sara Ruddick calls "maternal thinking."[25] A child of war herself, Chafia speaks of the need to protect children from war, to work towards a non-violent, humane world, and to change societal attitudes that lead to individual and collective forms of madness:

> Faire respecter sérieusement les droits des enfants, ce serait changer la face du monde. . . . Nous sommes bien obligés, nous les femmes, de travailler à ce que ce monde-là devienne meilleur, si nous voulons être conséquentes avec nous-mêmes, si nous voulons que nos accouchements et notre travail aient un sens (Ghalem 79).
>
> [Ensuring children's rights are respected would be to change the face of the world. . . . As women, we really have to work to make the world a better place if we want to be consistent in our actions, if we want our giving birth and our labor to have any meaning.]

By proposing such a goal, Chafia gives mothers a role that goes beyond the confines of the home and which women themselves have defined. This role places them squarely on the side of children and poets, and suggests mothers and daughters can work together on a common script for the future in which the emphasis is on change rather than reproduction.

The strong statement on reconciliation at the end of *Les Jardins de cristal* could serve as an epigraph to this essay and to the history of mother-daughter relations in general: "Le chemin aura été terrible. Il aura d'abord fallu nous renier toutes deux avant de nous retrouver" (Ghalem 136). [The road traveled will have been terrible. We both had to disown each other before finding one another again.] The four novels discussed portray the difficulties and the rewards of bringing about such a reconciliation. Taken together, they indicate the direction to be followed and provide compelling reasons for refiguring the mother-daughter relationship. In particular, their emphasis on working together as women posits that healthier, less destructive mother-daughter relations are fundamental to creating new familial and societal structures. In this fashion, they suggest, the "noyau extrêmement explosif" (Irigaray 1981, 86) [the highly explosive nucleus] --- the mother-daughter team --- could have a transformative effect on both individual women's lives and on society at large.

Works Cited and Bibliography

Badinter, Elisabeth. *Mother Love: Myth and Reality*. New York: Macmillan, 1981.

Chen, Ying. *L'Ingratitude*. Montreal: Leméac, 1995.

Chesler, Phyllis. *Women and Madness*. New York: Doubleday, 1972.

Chodorow, Nancy. *The Reproduction of Mothering: Psychoanalysis and the Sociology of Gender*. Berkeley: University of California Press, 1978.

Dally, Ann. *Inventing Motherhood: The Consequences of an Ideal*. New York: Schocken Press, 1983.

Daly, Brenda O., and Maureen T. Reddy, Editors. *Narrating Mothers: Theorizing Maternal Subjectivities*. Knoxville: University of Tennessee Press, 1991.

Davidson, Cathy, and E. M. Broner, Editors. *The Lost Tradition : Mothers and Daughters in Literature*. New York: Frederick Ungar, 1980.

Ghalem, Nadia. *Les Jardins de cristal*. Quebec: Hurtubise HMH, 1981.

Foucault, Michel. *Madness and Civilization: A History of Insanity in the Age of Reason*. Translated by Richard Howard. New York: Pantheon, 1965.

Garner, Shirley Nelson, Claire Kahane, and Madelon Sprengnether. *The (M)other Tongue: Essays in Psychoanalytic Interpretation*. Ithaca: Cornell University Press, 1985.

Gould, Karen. "Refiguring the Mother: Quebec Women Writers in the 80s." *International Journal of Canadian Studies* 6 (Fall 1992): 113-125.

Hirsch, Marianne. *The Mother/Daughter Plot: Narrative, Psychoanalysis, Feminism*. Bloomington: Indiana University Press, 1989.

Irigaray, Luce. *Et l'une ne bouge pas sans l'autre*. Paris: Minuit, 1979.

_____. *Le Corps-à-corps, avec la mère*. Montreal: Editions de la Pleine Lune, 1981.

Kaplan, Ann E. *Motherhood and Representation: The Mother in Popular Culture and Melodrama*. London: Routledge, 1992.

Kristeva, Julia. *Polylogue*. Paris: Seuil, 1977.

LaRue, Monique. "La Mère, aujourd'hui." *La Nouvelle Barre du Jour* 116 (1982): 51-5.

Lequin, Lucie. "L'Épreuve de l'exil et la traversée des frontières: des voix de femmes." *Québec Studies* 14 (1992): 31-39.

_____ and Maïr Verthuy, Editors. *Multi-culture multi-écriture: la voix migrante en France et au Québec*. Paris: L'Harmattan, 1996.

Nepveu, Pierre. *L'Ecologie du réel*. Montreal: Boréal, 1988.

Plath, Sylvia. *The Bell Jar*. New York: Harper and Row, 1971.

Rich, Adrienne. *Of Woman Born: Motherhood as Experience and Institution*. New York: W.W. Norton, 1976.

Ruddick, Sara. *Maternal Thinking: Toward a Politics of Peace*. Boston: Beacon Press, 1989.

Saad, Tiziana Beccarelli. *Vers l'Amérique*. Montreal: Triptyque, 1988.

Showalter, Elaine. *The Female Malady: Women, Madness, and English Culture, 1830-1980.* New York: Pantheon Books, 1985.

_____. *The New Feminist Criticism.* New York: Pantheon Books, 1986.

Simon, Sherry and David Leahy. "La Recherche au Québec portant sur l'écriture ethnique." *Ethnicity and Culture in Canada.* Edited by J.V. Berry and J.A. Laponce. Toronto: University of Toronto Press, 1994.

Smart, Patricia. *Writing in the Father's House: The Emergence of the Feminine in the Quebec Literary Tradition.* Toronto: University of Toronto Press, 1991. (Author's translation of *Ecrire dans la maison du pére,* 1988.)

Thompson, Elizabeth. *The Pioneer Woman: A Canadian Character Type.* Montreal: McGill-Queen's University Press, 1991.

Ussher, Jane M. *Women's Madness: Misogyny or Mental Illness?* Amherst: University of Massachusetts Press, 1991.

Yalom, Marilyn. *Maternity, Mortality, and the Literature of Madness.* University Park: Pennsylvania State University Press, 1985.

Zagolin, Bianca. *Une Femme à la fenêtre.* Paris: Robert Laffont, 1988.

Additional Reading:

Saint-Martin, Lori. "Le Corps et la fiction à réinventer: metamorphoses de la maternité dans l'écriture des femmes au Québec." *Recherches féministes* 7.2 (1994): 115-134.

Endnotes

1. "Toute notre culture repose sur le meurtre de la mère" (Irigaray 1981, 81). [Our whole culture is founded on matricide.]

2. "'Matrophobia,' as the poet Lynn Sukenick has termed it, is the fear not of one's mother or of motherhood but of *becoming one's mother*" (Rich 235).

3. Theoretical texts that focus on the mother include: *The Reproduction of Mothering* (Chodorow), *Of Woman Born: Motherhood as Institution and Experience* (Rich), *The (M)other Tongue: Essays in Feminist Psychoanalysis* (Garner, Kahane and Sprengnether), *The Lost Tradition: Mothers and Daughters in Literature* (Davidson and Bröner), *Inventing Motherhood: The Consequences of an Ideal* (Dally), *Mother Love: Myth and Reality* (Badinter), *Motherhood and Representation* (Kaplan), *Narrating Mothers* (Daly and Reddy), *Polylogue* (Kristeva), *Et l'une ne bouge pas sans l'autre* (Irigaray), and *Le Corps-à-corps, avec la mère* (Irigaray).

4. Daughter-centered texts cited by Gould include the works of feminist writers such as Marie-Claire Blais, Louky Bersianik, France Théoret, Madeleine Gagnon, and Jovette Marchessault.

5. For a discussion of recent novels written from the perspective of the mother, see Gould's "Refiguring the Mother: Quebec Women Writers in the 80s."

6. "The emergence of an ethnic voice in Quebec literature is a relatively recent phenomenon. . . . it was only in the 1980s that there came into critical existence a category designating authors of immigrant or culturally diverse origins" (Simon, Leahy 387). For a discussion of this body of literature, see, for example, "L'Épreuve de l'exil et la traversée des frontières: des voix de femmes" (Lucie Lequin), *L'Écologie du réel* (Pierre Nepveu), *Multi-culture multi-écriture* (Lucie Lequin and Maïr Verthuy), and "La recherche au Québec portant sur l'écriture ethnique" (Sherry Simon and David Leahy).

7. "Je pense qu'il est nécessaire aussi, pour ne pas être complices du meurtre de la mère, que nous affirmions qu'il existe une généalogie de femmes. Généalogie de femmes dans notre famille: après tout, nous avons une mère, une grand-mère, une arrière grand-mère, des filles. Essayons de nous situer pour conquérir et garder notre identité dans cette généalogie féminine" (Irigaray 1981, 30). [If we are not to become accomplices of matricide, I believe it is necessary for us to affirm the existence of a genealogy of women. Of a genealogy of women in our own families: after all, we have mothers, grandmothers, great-grandmothers, daughters. Let us try to situate ourselves in this female genealogy in order to conquer and to keep our identity.]

8. The expression the "Father's House" is from the title of Patricia Smart's *Writing in the Father's House: The Emergence of the Feminine in the Quebec Literary Tradition.*

9. Teresa's hesitation to return to Italy is explained by her fear of being silenced and of being subjected to the authority of the men in her family: "rentrer au pays, c'est réapprendre à se taire quand l'homme parle" (Saad 42). [Returning home means learning once again to keep silent when man speaks.]

10. "L'Amérique, c'était le paradis. C'était la promesse de tout ce qui était encore possible. Sortir de la misère, de la crasse, du travail des champs. Ben, je l'ai pas trouvé encore moi, l'Amérique" (Saad 24). [America was paradise. It was the promise of everything that was still possible. Of getting away from poverty, squalor, work in the fields. Well --- I haven't reached America yet.]

11. The relationship Mia finds the most problematic is the one with her father of whom she is ashamed.

12. In this sense, Aurore is Zagolin's version of "the pioneer woman." Elizabeth Thompson's analysis of this character type emphasizes the change in nature of the frontier over time --- "The frontier is redefined several times, and with the redefinition comes a corresponding change in the nature of the pioneering process (or in the pioneer woman's interaction with the frontier)" (7). Aurore's frontier is both physical and psychological, a real place and an internal territory.

13. "Le désir d'elle, son désir à elle, voilà ce que doit interdire la loi du père --- de tous les pères. Pères de familles, pères de nations, pères-médecins, pères-curés, pères-professeurs. Moraux ou immoraux. Toujours, ils interviennent pour censurer, refouler . . . le désir de la mère" (Irigaray 1981, 15). [Desire of her, her own desire, this is what the law of the father --- of all fathers --- has to prohibit. Fathers of families, fathers of nations, doctor-fathers, religious fathers, teacher-fathers. Be they moral or immoral. They always intervene to censure, to repress, desire of the mother.]

14. Aurore does not abandon her role as mother in favor of that of mistress: "il n'était pas question pour Aurore de se dépouiller de sa maternité; pas un instant n'aurait-elle songé à se soustraire aux impératifs de ce rôle" (Zagolin 73). [There was no question of Aurore abandoning motherhood; she would not for one moment have thought of shirking the obligations of that role.]

15. "Et Sébastien était cet objet qui lui avait restitué sa place au coeur des choses, où elle pouvait respirer, connaître, grandir sans peur, s'appeler de son nom, Aurore" (Zagolin 80). [And Sébastien was the thing that had given her back her place at the center of life, a place where she could breathe, learn, grow without being afraid, call herself by her name, Aurore.]

16. Although Yan-zi has enough sleeping tablets to kill herself, and engages in suicidal fantasies in which she imagines her death and her jubilant reactions to her mother's suffering, her death is the result of an accident: she is run over by a truck as she tries to escape from Chun, who she believes has been sent by her mother to look for her.

17. "Je pensais que c'était un peu à cause de lui que maman et moi nous entendions comme le feu et l'eau. S'il avait été moins professeur d'université, s'il s'était soucié autant de ce qu'il y avait sur notre table à manger que de ce qui se passait au Vietnam ou en Yougoslavie, s'il était allé plus souvent au marché qu'au musée, s'il avait daigné se montrer un peu plus attentif à maman... maman aurait été moins dépendante de ma présence et de ma vertu. Si seulement papa avait pu partager un peu avec moi l'énorme responsabilité de rendre heureuse cette femme qui avait tant fait pour moi et pour lui, j'aurais pu mieux respirer et peut-être vivre plus longtemps" (Chen 30). [I thought it was partly because of him that Mama and I got along like fire and water. If he had been less of a university professor, if he had worried as much about what we had to eat on our table as he worried about what was happening in Vietnam or Yugoslavia, if he had gone to the market more often than he went to the museum, if he had deigned to be a bit more attentive to Mama's needs...Mama would have been less dependent on my presence and my virtue. If only papa had shared with me a little the huge responsibility of making the woman who had done so much for him and for me happy, I would have been able to breathe more easily and perhaps live longer.]

18. "Les traîtres à leur mère continueront, morts comme vivants, à vagabonder, à se voir exclus du cycle de la vie, à être partout et nulle part. A ne pas être" (Chen 129). [Those who betray their mothers will continue --- in life and in death --- to wander aimlessly, to be excluded from the cycle of life, to be everywhere and nowhere. To not be.]

19. Yalom observes that "Twentieth-century women writers have appropriated literary insanity for their own ends and have endowed it with specifically female parameters" (2).

20. Chafia thus sets up her own paradigm in which those who represent law and order stand in oposition to those equated with "la folie" --- "vous qui êtes du côté de la loi et de l'ordre et de ce réalisme sec, tellement moins intéressant que ma folie" (Ghalem 68). [You who are on the side of law and order and dry realism, which is far less interesting than my madness.]

21. Foucault, for example, examines the use of psychiatric medicine as a form of social regulation. For a discussion of the patriarchal nature of psychiatric treatment, see Phyllis Chesler (*Women and Madness*), Showalter (*The Female Malady*), and Jane M. Ussher (*Women's Madness: Misogyny or Mental Illness*).

[22] "Je vous l'ai déjà dit, je suis comme une grenouille dans un jardin de cristal. Vous m'avez entourée de vos ronces acérées et, chaque fois que je me débats, les échardes coupantes me trouent les chairs. Vous avez voulu que ma révolte soit longuement et insidieusement douloureuse" (Ghalem 72). [I've already told you, I'm like a frog in a crystal garden. You have surrounded me with your pointed thorns and every time I try to move, their sharp splinters cut into my flesh. You wanted my rebellion to be insidiously long and painful.]

[23] Several images suggest the presence of the mother in herself: "Mais je vous défie de me faire oublier ce qui court dans mes veines. On dirait que c'est un fluide que ma mère m'a légué" (Ghalem 76). [But I defy you to make me forget what flows in my veins --- it appears to be a liquid my mother bequeathed me.]

[24] "Au bout des années de colère et de terreur, j'aurais voulu que s'étende sur le corps fatigué de cette femme une vague de tendresse qui l'aurait couverte de douceur. Pour qu'elle sache enfin que sa vie n'avait pas été tout à fait inutile" (Ghalem 117). [At the end of the ysears of anger and terror, I would have liked a wave of tenderness to spread out over the tired body of this woman and cover her with gentleness . So that she would finally know her life had not been completely in vain.]

[25] "Maternal Thinking" is the title of Ruddick's book: *Maternal Thinking: Towards a Politics of Peace*. Ruddick takes the caregiving associated with mothering as a model for political action in which mothers' love for their children is extended to a concern for humanity in general.

Latin American Literature in Canada and Quebec: A Genesis?

Peter Klaus
Freie Universität (FU Berlin), Berlin, Germany

La chaleur moite d'autre fois n'existe que dans ma mémoire.
Ici les fleurs de givre couvrent les vitres d'une dentelle épaisse, grise...
Sergio Kokis, Le Pavillon des Miroirs, 18
[The damp heat of another time exists only in my memory.
Here flowers of frost cover the windowpanes with a thick, grey lace.]

In her collection of stories, suggestively entitled *Les Aurores montréales* [Montreal Dawns], Monique Proulx points to the new reality of the imaginary universes of *métissage*, a phenomenon recently apparent in Québécois literature, as well as in Anglophone Canadian literature.

Indeed, Proulx dedicated five stories in the collection to different (visible) minority groups in Quebec. Three texts are specifically addressed to Québécois writers in these groups, "Jaune et blanc" [Yellow and White] to Ying Chen, "Rose et blanc" [Pink and White] to Marco Micone, and "Noir et blanc" [Black and White] to Dany Laferrière. Two stories provide a kind of frame for the collection: the first, "Gris et blanc" [Grey and White], deals with the fate of a Latin American immigrant; one of the last, "Rouge et blanc" [Red and White], involves Aataensic, mother of all humans, an allusion to Amerindian, and specifically to Huron, mythology. In fact, this text ends with the words "Help me, oh, Aataentsic, to remain a human being ..." (Proulx 196).

Monique Proulx, author of *Homme invisible à la fenêtre* [Invisible Man at the Window] among other works, is, to my knowledge, the first Québécois writer to deal so explicitly with the composite (or should one say "heterogeneous"?) picture of Québécois society, the identity debate in Québécois literature, and the increasingly noticeable, often remarkable, contribution of writers of origins other than *pure laine* or *de souche*. Montreal, the new Babel, is the site of the *métissages* Proulx brings to our attention. The birth of an immigrant voice, or of *"écriture migrante"* (migratory writing), forces readers to look again at their small universe through different eyes, and to redefine exoticism.[1] It is precisely in "Babel prise deux, ou nous avons tous découvert l'Amérique" [Babel, take two, or we all discovered America] that Fatima, the heroine of this novel by Francine Noel is chagrined by the integration of the Neo-Québécois in her society (and also by the future of the French language).[2] But does Quebec really hope to integrate an authentic literature, the origins of which are not Québécois?

Certainly the identity debate in Quebec would lose its flavor without the existence of "hyphenated identities". The Québécois themselves have been constrained to use composite identities in order to work through the tangle of ethnographic neologisms. These terminology clusters have multiplied in recent years, but some of them, in fact, belong to the history of Canada and Quebec. Notions such as French Canadian, or French-speaking Canadian translate, in the first case, a certain desire for hyper-specificity, and in the second case a need for identification.

Most recently, the term Neo-Québécois has emerged as a clear designation for the immigrant from elsewhere, the term Québécois no longer bearing the necessary clarity. In a lecture presented at the University of Montreal, the poet Gilles Marcotte, who was also a professor of literature for many years at the Université de Montréal, made the same ironic point, speaking of the "native-born French-speaking Québécois".

What then can we say about this most recent arrival on the literary scene, known as Latin American Canadian literature, or Canadian Latin American literature, or Québécois Latin American, or even Latin Québécois? These hybrid neologisms bring out a compelling cultural reality which is, in part, the general phenomenon of immigrants finding their voice in literature, and in part, a real emergence of a Latin American literary presence in Canada, and specifically in Quebec. Though it is often the case that Haiti is included in such discussions, Haitian Québécois literature is omitted from this essay, if only because at present, at least half of Haitian literature comes from the diaspora, and of that half, the better part is from Montreal. On the other hand, the use of the term Latino-Québécois in this essay refers to any immigrant to Quebec from a Central or South American country.

Jorge Etcheverry, the Chilean writer who has been a resident of Quebec since 1975, has thematized a universal drama of our time in his poem "Exilés/The Exiled", published in Spanish and English in a 1993 edition of *Ruptures: La Revue des 3 Amériques*.[3] Rather than treating the problem of exile as an abstract matter, Etcheverry presents the specific suffering of the individual living in that existential state. His words reflect the confusion and sadness of those who have stayed at home as much as they convey the trauma of those who have been persecuted in their own land.

Faces strained by anxiety, nights spent in a constant state of fear rather than in the healing comfort of dreams, days that pass like nightmares: these are the topics in this poem that continually and metaphorically push it beyond a simple reference to Chilean politics after the fall of Allende in September 1973. In their own country, those being persecuted are "free" as birds, which is to say that they are outlaws. For as birds, they are easy prey for hunters. Persecution, torture, certain death make their lives at home in their own country impossible. Their only escape is to put down roots elsewhere, far from home. The risk-laden result of such a strategy is to be uprooted culturally and linguistically, to be without any real country in the end, without any true homeland, and to be forced to base the future on a foundation of uncertainties and unknowns.

Etcheverry's poem is one of the most recent examples of Latino-Canadian literature, and its publication in *Ruptures*, which is directed by a Haitian poet living in Montreal, situates it in the context of the current literary scene in Canada, more particularly, in Montreal. It also attests to the major contribution of Chileans in Canada to the current literary life of their host country.

Canada and Quebec absorbed the first waves of massive Latin American immigration following the fall of Allende and the establishment of a military dictatorship in Chile. Approximately 40,000 Chileans entered Canada, and of those, 8,000 came to Quebec, where they formed the province's largest and most active group of Latin American refugees. Their number was subsequently increased by sizable groups of Argentines, Salvadoreans, Nicaraguans, Guatamalans and Peruvians.[4]

To appreciate the specific impact of Latin American immigration in Quebec, it is helpful to keep in mind that, in contrast with other immigrant groups, and with the exception of Brazilians, Latin American immigrants, whatever their country of origin, all speak and write Spanish.

A second distinguishing characteristic is the fact that the greater proportion of the members of this immigrant group are political refugees. By and large, they belong to the political left of their respective countries of origin, where they were politically and socially active, and suffered as a consequence from various military dictatorships and civil wars. Many of them chose to come to Quebec specifically for its language and culture, and with few exceptions, they have been assimilated into their Francophone surroundings. However, they continue to write either in Spanish, or in both French and Spanish.

A third common feature of this group is the prestige, proliferation and high level of the arts, particularly of literature, in the countries from which the members come. Many Latin American immigrants were already recognized writers in their homeland. This fact is not without importance for their subsequent development as writers in Canadian or Québécois exile, for the literature they produce is thus placed in a tradition with a substantial history.

The Canadian critic Lake Sagaris has argued that an underdeveloped economy such as that of many South American countries does not necessarily yield a backward culture.[5] She cites as evidence the two Nobel Prizes awarded to Chileans, one to Gabriela Mistral, the first woman and the first Latin American author to receive this distinction, in 1945; and a second to Pablo Neruda in 1971. During the 70s, in the initial years of their residence in Quebec, the preferred genre of immigrant Latin American writers was poetry, a penchant also noticeable in early Haitian writing during the 60s in Montreal. But since that time, Hugh Hazelton[6] has written of a true Latino-Québécois literature. In what sense might this be understood?

At present, there are approximately 40 Latin American writers living in Montreal. They work in a broad range of literary genres, from poetry to short narrative, to novels and thrillers to children's books, and, in the case of Alberto Kurapel, even to performance theatre. As early as 1978, Chilean writers in exile created a literary platform for themselves with the magazine *Literatura Chilena en el Exilio* [Chilean Literature in Exile], originally based in California, and many writers made a name for themselves through this publication. But this was only a beginning. Associations were created, among them most notably the Chilean Association of Montreal/Association Chilienne de Montréal. This association established the publishing house of Cordillera in 1978, which published the first anthology of Chilean literature in Canada in 1982.[7]

Currently, Hispanophone newspapers such as *Toronto Latino* in Toronto and *El Correo* in Montreal also contribute to the awareness and distribution of Latino-Canadian or Latino-Québécois literature. They are supported by two literary Hispanophone magazines, *Sur* [South], under the direction of Tito Alvarado, and *La Botella Verde* [The Green Bottle], published by Jorge Cancino, both based in Montreal. Aside from textual production, activities of all kinds --- readings, meetings, intercultural celebration weeks, the establishment of bookstores specializing in Hispanophone literature, and small publishing houses --- sustain the cultural presence of Latin Americans in Quebec. Furthermore, the publication of French language anthologies of Latino-American literature in Montreal introduce readers to Latino-American writers living in Quebec, or familiarize Québécois readers with Latin America through poetry.[8] It is, of course, important to note that such undertakings can be ephemeral. *Ruptures*, the magazine that published Etcheverry's seminal poem, was only recently forced to cease publishing, and other magazines and publishing houses may, in fact, suffer the same fate. Nonetheless, Hazelton's claim that there is a Latino-Québécois literature is borne out by the high degree of literary activity and the peripheral cultural expressions that are a part of it.

Chilean prose written in Canada first appeared in 1980 in a special edition of *Canadian Fiction Magazine*. Chile had long been a subject of fascination for Canadian writers, perhaps because of Nobel prizewinner Pablo Neruda, perhaps also because many writers feel that the two countries share several features, dictatorship aside, of course. In fact, according to Lake Sagaris, it was the dictatorship of Pinochet itself that underlies the "greatest exchange of Chilean and Canadian experience in the history of both countries."[9] For several Canadian writers continued to be a solid presence in Chile during Pinochet's regime. As an example, Canadian poets Gary Geddes, Pat Lane, Lorna Crozier and Mary Di Michele journeyed to Santiago in September 1987 in the final chapter of a 25-year odyssey of Canadian poetry in Chile. For Di Michele, the Italo-Canadian poet from Montreal, the most exotic aspect of Chileans was the degree to which poetry seemed their natural dialect.[10]

The experience of these Canadian writers and the exile suffered by their Chilean counterparts in Canada had concrete results: a Spanish-English anthology entitled *Chilean Writers in Canada*, published by Naìn Gomez in 1982, and a double edition of *Canadian Fiction Magazine*, devoted to Latin American writers in Canada in 1987. Of the 13 writers featured, 8 were Chilean. In his preface, Geoffrey Hancock, editor of *Canadian Fiction Magazine*, observes, "This issue of *Canadian Fiction Magazine* asks that these writers be considered part of the revolution within contemporary Canadian literature and thought. How can we read these fictions within a Canadian context? How do these writings affect our 'reading' of Canadian fiction and criticism?"[11] Nor was it a coincidence that Lake Sagaris entitled her article "The Chile-Canada Connection, or The Future of Fiction" (*Canadian Fiction Magazine*, 67/68, 1989), and another article, this one published in a special edition of *Canadian Literature/Littérature Canadienne* 142/143, 1994, "Countries like Drawbridges: Chilean-Canadian Writing Today."

The features and problems dealt with by Hancock and Sagaris have to do, of course, with English Canada, but they concern Quebec, as well. The revolution Hancock is talking about occurs in Quebec, too, and I venture to suggest that one of the catalysts is Chile and Chilean writers in exile. For Canada, Chile became part of the process of identifying with the victimized of the world, a concern often expressed through the struggle for the rights of the individual. In Sagaris's opinion, this reciprocal involvement contributed to a reinforcement of Canadian democracy.

From another point of view, the position of the individual in exile made possible the genesis of a literature of involvement, impossible in the countries under dictatorship. As an example, *Pièges* [Traps], a novel by Gloria Escomel published in 1992 by Boréal, might be considered a kind of literature of combat against dictatorship and government-sponsored misinformation of the public. In the novel, the author, who was born in Montevideo, and reported frequently from Uruguay, Chile and Argentina, makes a plea for democracy, defends militantism and social obligation.

As another example, the Chilean Marilù Mallet has dealt principally with the anxieties of persecuted individuals, and the traumas of torture, death and exile. Her two prose works, *Les Compagnons de l'horloge-pointeuse* [Timeclock Companions] and *Miami Trip*, published in Montreal in 1981 and 1986 respectively, were written first in Spanish, then published in French. Particularly in the second work, she depicts the position of the exiled individual in the host country, and the accompanying cultural and linguistic uprooting. The integration of the Latin American immigrant (or any immigrant, it appears) is made difficult by the weight of the past, and nightmarish obsessions that are reflected in the very act of learning the language of the new country, that indispensable act without which there is no integration. In the Kafkaesque title of the story "La Mutation" [The Mutation], the reader is given a foretaste of the situation confronting a family of Latin American immigrants in Montreal. To facilitate the linguistic and cultural integration of their three year-old son Pepito, his parents enroll him in a Francophone day care center. Imagine their surprise when two years later they realize that Pepito is only able to emit nasalized, incomprehensible sounds. They consult various doctors who make scientific diagnoses, one more upsetting than the other. According to one of these, the boy's problems were caused by prenatal trauma; according to another, they were the consequences of torture and electric shock his father experienced under the dictatorship in his home country. Other elements are added to this one: the parents both have dark hair, but Pepito is blond and has a deformed foot. As a result, the father and mother argue over who is responsible for the situation, who is at fault, who is perhaps even guilty. But the conclusion turns out to be much more positive than this rather monstrous scenario. In the Francophone day care center, which is in fact multilingual and multicultural, and therefore a faithful reflection of Montreal society, Pepito makes friends with a little boy whose mother tongue is Hungarian. And so he learns Hungarian, "that devil of a nasal language".[12] The moral of the story is that learning foreign languages is good, and is entrusted with a sizable social function, a kind of royal road to success.

Alberto Kurapel, a Chilean who has lived in Montreal since 1970, has made a substantial impression on the Québécois theatre scene since founding the Compagnie des Arts Exilio in Montreal in 1981. His conception of exile and integration is quite different from that of Escomel and Mallet. Using theatre as an instrument, he has placed the concern of the exiled individual with his existential situation at the center of attention. Alfonso de Toro has called Kurapel's work "théâtre multimédia interspectaculaire post-moderne" (interspectacular post-modern multimedia theatre).[13] Kurapel uses two languages, Spanish and French, simultaneously in his productions. With him, language, or rather languages, become the key problem of exile and exiled individuals. By having each text repeated in his plays in Spanish and in French, with no transition, he represents what for him is the true condition of exile and those in exile, which is to say, "une conscience fragmentée" [a fragmented consciousness][14]. He describes his theatre as a "Latin American Performance of Exile,"[15] theatrical performance itself defined as a kind of exile.

Exile is most certainly a central concern of all immigrant literature. An original manner of understanding this phenomenon has been demonstrated with great success by Sergio Kokis. A painter and psychologist from Brazil, Kokis lived in Paris, before coming to Quebec about 20 years ago. His first novel, *Le Pavillon des miroirs* [The House of Mirrors], published in French in Montreal in 1995, met immediately with a success that has since been unequalled, winning four prizes: the Grand prix du Livre de Montréal in 1994, the Prix de l'Académie des Lettres du Québec also in 1994, the Prix Québec-Paris and the Prix Littéraire Desjardins du Roman, both in 1995. Such a sweep of awards is unprecedented, and merits close attention, for the honors do not simply recognize a good novel. They also pay homage to that entire generation of immigrants who, by adding their particular and unique ideas, are contributing to the fashioning and metamorphoses of Québécois literature.

Le Pavillon des miroirs has a shifting story line. One narrative recounts the past of the young narrator who grew up in Rio de Janeiro under incredibly difficult conditions. The second narrative is centered on the thoughts of a painter exiled in some unnamed northern country which the reader easily imagines to be Quebec. The novel, unfolding in a tropical context rich with color, is a kind of initiatory narrative, punctuated with thoughts on the fate of the exiled individual and on the function of language.

The language problems the narrator encounters in Brazil would not surprise a Québécois of today. His father vaunts the merits of English, which he associates with success and modernity (Kokis 86). According to him, even immigrants without resources can succeed, though they are not Americans (Kokis 119). A second element that suggests a similarity between Quebec and Brazil is religion. For the narrator's mother, "les choses de la religion, c'est comme l'anglais pour mon père: the key to success" [things having to do with religion is like English for my father: the key to success]. He adds: Heureusement, mon père n'aime pas les curés. Il est protestant, il n'aime pas les pasteurs non plus, ni rien qui traite de la religion" (Kokis 90) [fortunately, my father doesn't like priests. He's Protestant, he doesn't like ministers either, or anything having to do with religion].

Returning to the set of problems dealing with the immigrant's language, Kokis's narrator observes that the immigrant has no language but the one he borrows (Kokis 70). To be exiled in a language, in one's own language: that is the experience of the narrator, who tells us that when he was still in school in Brazil, foreign languages seemed to him to be full of promises, ready to reveal the unknown (Kokis 167). And before having his own experiences as an exiled individual, he recalls his astonishment at hearing "...les vieux oncles de mon père, séniles, ravagés par l'alcool. Ils avaient perdu leur langue d'adoption, et ne parlaient désormais qu'un mélange de letton et d'allemand parsemé d'injures ou d'obscénités bien tropicales" (Kokis 282) [... my father's aging uncles, senile and ruined by alcohol. They had lost their adopted tongue, and could speak now only in a mixture of Latvian and German, sprinkled with insults and obscenities of a highly tropical nature]. This experience provokes the observation that now, he is always thinking in a foreign language "...parce que, avec le temps, elles se sont toutes mêlées. Ça devient une sorte de traduction, parfois fiction ou tricherie..." (Kokis 280) [because with time, (the languages) all become jumbled together. They became a kind of translation, sometimes fiction or trickery].

At first he felt like some exotic animal in a zoo. "...[S]achant que je viens de là-bas, ils (les visiteurs dans son atelier) bifurquent sur le carnaval ou la samba... Les belles plages, hein?... Les tristes tropiques. J'ai déjà passé une semaine à Acapulco, ou en Jamaïque, ou à un Club Méditerranée, je ne m'en souviens plus... Que répondre? Leur casser la gueule, me mettre à faire quelques pas de samba, ou violer sur-le-champ la femme du visiteur... C'est un dur métier, l'exil" (Kokis 48). [Knowing that I come from down there, the visitors to my studio launch into the Carnival or the samba... Nice beaches, right?... Sad tropics. I spent a week in Acapulco, or in Jamaica, or at a Club Med, I don't even remember anymore... What can I answer? Kick him in the face, start doing the samba, or rape his wife on the spot... It's a hard job, exile.] In the end, he is more conciliatory, noting that we are always a foreigner to someone, even if we are unaware of it. "...Au travail, dans la rue, je m'amusais à mon petit jeu, protégé désormais par l'uniforme impersonnel de l'immigration..." (Kokis 302). [At work, on the street, I played my little game, protected now by the impersonal uniform of immigration.]

These few examples from Kokis's novel demonstrate how the imagination of a writer from the south can contribute to the understanding of the revolution we have been discussing. Seeing the broad horizon of the Latin American literary production in Quebec and the rest of Canada, it is clear to what degree their contribution is significant in helping to better understand the Other. Quebec publishers have understood this, and, like the publishing house of VLB, which has published among other titles a detective story originally written in Argentine Spanish, are taking on increasing numbers of Latin American writers. The author of this work, Pablo Urbanyi, an Argentine of Hungarian background, is torn between old Europe and an America which is hardly Latin, insofar as he now lives in Ottawa. His second novel, *Un Revolver pour Mack* [A Revolver for Mack] is a parody of the classic whodunit that attempts to demystify the crime thriller, yet pay homage to it at the same time.

The contribution of Chilean writers, of Brazilian Sergio Kokis, and finally, of the Hungarian Argentine from Ottawa: what more is needed to give us an idea of the wealth of Latin American literary material in Quebec and Canada? Nor should we be surprised to learn that in the countries of origin of these authors, there is pronounced interest in learning about the Latin American literature of the diaspora, that there exist co-publications between Quebec, Canada and Chile, and that, for example, the distribution of books by these same authors is underwritten by a publishing house in Santiago. This cooperation is facilitated moreover by those writers who have returned to their countries after the re-establishment of democratic regimes.

Yet there remains a small matter which is an important issue. What is the reaction and response to this literature? In a talk entitled "L'Arpenteur et le navigateur"[16] [The Surveyor and the Navigator], Monique LaRue questions those Québécois writers who look with a critical eye upon the emergence of an immigrant literature. She criticizes above all their somewhat mean jealousy of the literary prizes awarded the works of immigrant writers. According to her, some Québécois writers see Québécois literature threatened in its homogeneity by immigrant authors. This attitude does not seem to take into account the entire evolution of Québécois literature since the 80s. Where would the literature of Quebec be today without authors such as Emile Ollivier, Marco Micone, Gérard Étienne, Ying Chen, Sergio Kokis and Alberto Kurapel, without poets such as Anthony Phelps, Joël des Rosiers or Saint-John Kauss? Some of these same immigrant authors have been featured for some years now in several anthologies of Québécois literature. When he was asked about the identity of the exiled individual, Leandro Urbina, the Chilean novelist from Montreal, responded, "I don't think writers have much identity ... Not like politicians who live on it. What is really important is to have an editor..."

Works Cited and Bibliography

Alvarado, Tito, et al. *La Présence d'une autre Amérique. Anthologie des écrivains latino-américains du Québec.* Montreal: Les Editions de la Naine Blanche, 1989.

Champagne, Christine. "Des Cahiers come preuve d'existence. Regards sur l'intimité comme sur le quotidien, les romans de Michèle Mailhot et Francine Noël laissent d'abord parler le 'je'." *Lettres québécoises. Revue de l'actualité littéraire.* No. 61, Printemps 1991, 21-22.

de Toro, Alfonso. "Alberto Kurapel, le Guanaco gaucho. Carta de ajuste ou nous n'avons plus besoin de calendrier." *Théâtre.* Montreal: Humanitas-Nouvelle Optique.

Etcheverry, Jorge. "Chilean Literature in Canada between the Coup and the Plebiscite." *Canadian Ethnic Studies/Etudes Ethniques Canadiennes.* XXI, 2, 1989, 53-62.

_____. "Exiliados/Exilés/Exiled." *Ruptures. La Revue des Trois Amériques.* Montreal: 1993.

Gomez, Mayte. "Infinite Signs. Alberto Kurapel and the Semiotics of Exile." *Canadian Literature/Littérature Canadienne.* 142/143, Fall/Winter 1994, 38-50.

Hazelton, Hugh. "La Littérature latino-québécoise en plein essor." *Impressions.* 10, 1991, 22-24.

_____. and Gary Geddes, Editors. *Compañeros. An Anthology of Writings about Latin America.* Dunvegan, Ontario: Cormorant Books, 1990.

Kokis, Sergio. *Le Pavillon des Miroirs.* Montreal: XYZ Editeur, 1995.

Kurapel, Alberto. "Le Langage de l'exil." *Exil et Fiction* [Exile and Fiction]. Under the direction of Gina Stoiciu and Axel Maugey. Montreal: Humanitas-Nouvelle Optique, 1992, 69-82.

LaRue, Monique. "L'Arpenteur et le navigateur." *Les Grandes Conférences.* Montreal: Editions Fides et CETUQ, Université de Montréal, 1996.

Mallet, Marilù. *Miami Trip. Nouvelles.* Montreal: Québec/Amérique, 1986.

Potvin, Claude. "La Nouvelle comme exercice de style." *Lettres québécoises. Revue de l'actualité littéraire.* No. 1976, 1994, 32.

Proulx, Monique. *Homme invisible à la fenêtre.* Montreal: Boréal, 1993.

Sagaris, Lake. "The Chile-Canada Connection, or the Future of Fiction." *Canadian Fiction Magazine.* 67/68, 1989, 234-255.

---. "Countries like Drawbridges. Chilean-Canadian Writing Today." *Canadian Literature/Littérature Canadienne.* 142/143, Fall/Winter, 1994, 12-20.

Urbanyi, Paolo. *Un Revolver pour Mack.* Montreal: VLB Editeur, 1992.

Additional Reading

Immigration and Ethnicity in Canada: Selected Proceedings of the 22nd Annual Conference of the Association for Canadian Studies. Montreal: Université du Québec à Montréal, 1995.

Massey, Irving. *Identity and Community: Reflections on English, Yiddish and French Literature in Canada.* Detroit: Wayne State University Press, 1994.

Monette, Pierre. *L'Immigrant Montréal.* Montreal: Triptyque, 1994.

Simon, Sherry, Editor. *Culture in Transit: Translating the Literature of Quebec.* Montreal: Véhicule Press, 1995.

Endnotes

1. Potvin 32.

2. Champagne 21-22.

3. *Exilés*

Ils nous ont dit qu'ils s'en allaient
Que très bientôt ils reviendraient

Mais nous savions en nous-mêmes
que nous ne verrions plus ces visages anxieux

aux pupilles dilatées par la peur
par des rêves impossibles

Ils auront fait pousser leurs racines au loin
bien loin de nous

Ils planteront leur semence en des terres de couleur
insoupçonnée
Saturées de parfums distincts et de sons incertains
Terres dont nous ne connaissons que le nom
et ne pouvons prononcer

Voyez-les à présent remonter le vol
comme une volée d'oiseaux épouvantés par la décharge du
chasseur!

Un vide semble s'installer au milieu des nôtres
Une génération plus courageuse qu'aucune autre
regard franc comme paumes ouvertes

celle qui fait ses valises
parcourt nos rues avec une nostalgie anticipée une dernière fois

Laissons pleurer les plus vieux
Réjouissons-nous pour ceux qui s'en vont
et ne verront point leurs ailes coupées
ni leurs yeux aveuglés

Qu'ils fleurissent comme mille fleurs en d'autres terres

Que soient leurs fils étrange fruit salutaire
Qu'ils sachent leur conter des histoires, le soir, avant de
s'endormir

Sur cette terre
Sur nous-mêmes
Sur ce qu'ils ont laissé.

-Jorge Etcheverry

[*The Exiled*

They told us they were going away
That very soon they would return

But we knew in our hearts
that we would see these anxious faces no more

not see the pupils dilated with fear
with impossible dreams

they will have put down their roots far away
far from us

they will plant their seed in lands
of unsuspected color
Saturated with distinct fragrances and uncertain sounds
Lands whose names we don't know
and cannot pronounce

see them now take wing
like a flight of birds frightened by the hunter's firing
gun!

An emptiness seems to settle in amongst our loved ones
A generation more courageous than any other
its expression as frank as open palms

the one that packs its bags
runs through our streets with an anticipated nostalgia one last time

Let's let the older ones cry
Let's be happy for those who are leaving

and won't see their clipped wings
or their blinded eyes

Let them flower like a thousand flowers in other lands
Let their sons be a strange and salutary fruit
Let them know how to tell them stories, in the evening, before falling asleep

About this land
About us
About what they left behind.]

4. Hazelton 22.

5. Sagaris 1989, 239.

6. Hazelton 1.

7. Etcheverry 55, 62.

8. I cite here only by way of examples the following: Tito Alvarado, *La Présence d'une autre Amérique. Anthologie des écrivains latino-américains du Québec,* Montreal: Les Editions de la naine blanche, 1989 [The Presence of an Other America. Anthology of Latin-American Writers of Quebec]; Hugh Hazelton and Gary Geddes, Editors, *Compañeros. An Anthology of Writings about Latin America* (Dunvegan, Ontario: Cormorant Books, 1990).

9. Sagaris 1994, 13.

10. Sagaris 1989, 245.

11. Sagaris 1989, 251.

12. Mallet 54.

13. See Alfonso de Toro's article, "Alberto Kurapel, le Guanaco gaucho. Carta de ajuste ou nous n'avons plus besoin de calendrier" [Alberto Kurapel, the Guacho Guanaco. Carta de ajuste, or We Don't Need a Calendar Anymore] in *Theatre* (Montreal: Humanitas-Nouvelle Optique, s.d.) for an explanation of this description.

14. Gomez 41.

15. Gomez 39.

16. LaRue 17.

17. Sagaris 1989, 18.

Contributors

Jean-François Chassay, *Professeur agrégé_* in the Department of Literary Studies at the *Université du Québec à Montréal*, has published several books, the most recent being *Les Ponts* (a novel, Montréal: Leméac, 1995); *L'ambiguïté américaine. La Représentation des Etats-Unis dans la littérature québécoise* (Montréal: XYZ Editeur, 1995); and *Robert Coover. L'écriture contre les mythes* (Paris: Belin, 1996). His research concerns sociocritical problems in literature, and the relationship between science and literature.

Ritt Deitz is Faculty Assistant in the Department of French and Italian at the University of Wisconsin at Madison. Aside from the novels of Jacques Poulin, his research interests include the films and autobiographical writings of filmmaker Jean Renoir.

Ramon Hathorn currently teaches dramatic arts at the University of Guelph in Ontario. He co-edited *Images of Louis Riel in Canadian Culture* with Patrick Holland, and has written for the *Oxford Companion to Canadian Literature.* He is the author of *Our Lady of the Snows: Sarah Bernhardt in Canada* (New York: Peter Lang, 1996).

Susan Ireland, Associate Professor of French at Grinnell College in Iowa, has written on *Beur* fiction, Monique LaRue, Madeleine Monette, Jacques Godbout, Jacques Roubaud, Tassadit Imache, and several Algerian women writers.

Peter Klaus, whose doctoral degree is in Romance Philology, holds the title of *Akademischer Rat und Lektor* at the *Freie Universität Berlin.* He is the editor of *Canada: Cultures et littératures* *immigrées (Neue Romania*, Vol. 18, 1997), and has written on Amerindian literature in contemporary Francophone Canada.

Janis L. Pallister, Distinguished Professor of Romance Languages and Graduate Enhancement Professor of French at Bowling Green State University in Ohio, is the author of *The Cinema of Quebec* (Associated University Press) and *French-Speaking Women Filmmakers: A Guide* (Associated University Press). She has also written on French Renaissance literature, and on African cinema and literature.

Susan L. Rosenstreich, Associate Professor of Foreign Languages at Dowling College, has written on articles on North American and North African Francophone literatures, and is a contributor to the *Dictionnaire des oeuvres littéraires du Québec*. She has also written on French and Italian Renaissance literatures.

Guy Teissier, *Maître de conférences* at the *Université François Rabelais* in Tours, France, is the author of several articles on Michel-Marc Bouchard, Dominic Champagne, Jean Giraudoux, Robert Lepage, Roland Lepage, and Michel Tremblay.

Index

—N—

—O—

—P—

—Q—

—R—

—S—

—T—

—V—

—W—

—Z—